CULTURES OF THE WORLD
Bosnia and Herzegovina

Cavendish
Square

New York

Published in 2021 by Cavendish Square Publishing, LLC
243 5th Avenue, Suite 136, New York, NY 10016

Library of Congress Cataloging-in-Publication Data

Names: King, David C., author. | Nevins, Debbie, author.
Title: Bosnia and Herzegovina / David C. King, Debbie Nevins.
Description: Third edition. | New York, NY : Cavendish Square Publishing,
   LLC, 2021. | Series: Cultures of the world | Includes bibliographical
   references and index.
Identifiers: LCCN 2020003281 (print) | LCCN 2020003282 (ebook) | ISBN
   9781502655875 (Library) | ISBN 9781502655882 (ebook)
Subjects: LCSH: Bosnia and Herzegovina--Juvenile literature.
Classification: LCC DR1660 .K56 2021 (print) | LCC DR1660 (ebook) | DDC
   949.742--dc23
LC record available at https://lccn.loc.gov/2020003281
LC ebook record available at https://lccn.loc.gov/2020003282

Editor, third edition: Debbie Nevins
Designer, third edition: Jessica Nevins

Find us on

CONTENTS

BOSNIA AND HERZEGOVINA TODAY

BOSNIA AND HERZEGOVINA MIGHT BE ONE OF THE MOST complicated countries in the world. It is a single sovereign state composed of two main parts—but they are not, as one might assume, Bosnia and Herzegovina. Geographically speaking, these are simply the names of two regions in the country. Bosnia takes up most of the country, but a smaller, southern region is known as Herzegovina. They have been together as one place since the year 1350, which seems long enough that they could have arrived at a single name, but it was not to be.

Much more importantly, Bosnia and Herzegovina (often abbreviated as BiH, or just called Bosnia for short) today is also made up of two main political entities, the Federation of Bosnia and Herzegovina (FBiH) and Republika Srpska (Serb Republic, or RS). They share one national capital, Sarajevo.

The two parts are, in turn, populated by the country's three main ethnic-religious groups—the Bosniaks, the Croats, and the Serbs. The Bosniaks are Muslims, the Croats are Roman Catholics, and the Serbs are Eastern Orthodox Christians. They are all ethnically the same; all are Slavs. These three groups fought a dreadful three-way civil

ETNIČKA KARTA BOSNE I HERCEGOVINE

war in the early 1990s. The two parts of the country were then established and legalized in the peace agreement that ended that war.

The country was divided in half—not geometrically, but in terms of percentage of land area. One part became the Federation, with a Bosniak and Croat population. The other became the Republika, made up almost entirely of Bosnian Serbs. Together, the two parts are the nation of Bosnia and Herzegovina, and all the people living there, regardless of identity or religion, are Bosnians.

In addition to the two main parts, there is a small, neutral, ethnically mixed part of BiH called the Brcko (BRITCH-ko) District. If all this seems complicated, it is. The government structure is even more so. Three presidents—one from each ethnic-religious group—share the presidency for eight-month rotations in a four-year term.

Bosnia and Herzegovina is in the Balkan region of south-central Europe. Its immediate neighbors are Croatia, Montenegro, and Serbia. Throughout much of the 20th century, along with those neighbors and several others, it was part of a larger country, Yugoslavia. From 1945 to 1990, Yugoslavia was a communist country. Then, it broke apart, in concert with the fall of communism in the Soviet Union and Eastern Europe.

In September 2019, bullet holes still pockmark the sides of buildings in Sarajevo.

For Bosnians, the rush to freedom almost immediately triggered a civil war from 1992–1995. It was one of a series of interconnected conflicts that tore apart the former Yugoslavia. The cost of the Bosnian war was enormous. Thousands were killed, and thousands more were maimed for life; cities like Sarajevo and Mostar were heavily damaged; entire towns and villages were destroyed; and nearly 2 million people became homeless refugees. The economy was brought to a standstill, with roughly half the workforce unemployed.

War is never pretty, but this one featured an astonishing number of war crimes against innocent civilians. In three short years, genocide and crimes against humanity were perpetrated in Bosnia in horrors reminiscent of World War II.

The war led to far-reaching changes in people's way of living and even their way of thinking. The demographic face of Bosnia shifted tremendously as the three ethnic-religious groups lost the trust they once had in one another. Political leaders today increase the division by supporting cultural projects that lead each group to regard itself as inherently different from the others.

Thus, today's Bosnia and Herzegovina has a great deal of tumultuous baggage dragging it down. The passions that ignited the war still lie just under the surface of today's uneasy peace. Such a brutal war cannot be easily swept away into the past. Peace is paramount, of course, but then must come justice.

The International Criminal Tribunal for the Former Yugoslavia (ICTY), a United Nations (UN) court of law in The Hague, Netherlands, tried to administer that justice. Established in 1993, even before the war ended, the court provided victims an opportunity to give testimony. War criminals, including Slobodan Milosevic, the former president of Yugoslavia, were rounded up and made to face justice. Most of the cases relating to Bosnia dealt with crimes committed by Serbs and Bosnian Serbs, but the tribunal investigated crimes by all ethnic groups, also convicting Croats and Bosnian Muslims. Charges were brought against a total of 161 people before the tribunal officially closed in 2017.

Is reconciliation possible? Looking ahead, many Bosnians wonder what the future will hold. Will BiH remain as it is, one country with two segregated parts held together with the glue of a patchy peace agreement? After all, the General Framework Agreement for Peace in Bosnia and Herzegovina,

A cautionary message in graffiti adorns a rock near the Old Bridge in the city of Mostar, Bosnia and Herzegovina.

signed by the leaders of Croatia, Serbia, and Bosnia in Dayton, Ohio, in November 1995, is nobody's idea of a perfect solution.

The Federation of BiH looks to Europe and the West. It hopes to join the European Union (EU), and the country BiH as a whole has taken steps to begin the process. However, RS is less enthusiastic about aligning with Europe. It looks to Russia, with which it shares the Eastern Orthodox religion. The leaders of the RS, particularly the current Serb member of the three-part BiH presidency, Milorad Dodik, favor having the RS break away from Bosnia and become its own separate country. Many Serbs would like to go further and join the RS to neighboring Serbia. Even in the Federation, the Croats and Bosniaks (another name for Bosnian Muslims) live largely segregated lives.

The international community has a lot at stake in Bosnia. The country receives substantial amounts of reconstruction assistance and humanitarian aid from governments and nongovernmental organizations around the world. US support, by way of the Support for Eastern European Democracy (SEED) Act of 1989, has accounted for around 20 to 25 percent of economic growth in Bosnia and Herzegovina. In 2018, the country received about $450 million in direct foreign investment.

Will all of this support pay off? For investors hoping to see a stable, multiethnic democracy emerge in BiH, the crystal ball seems foggy.

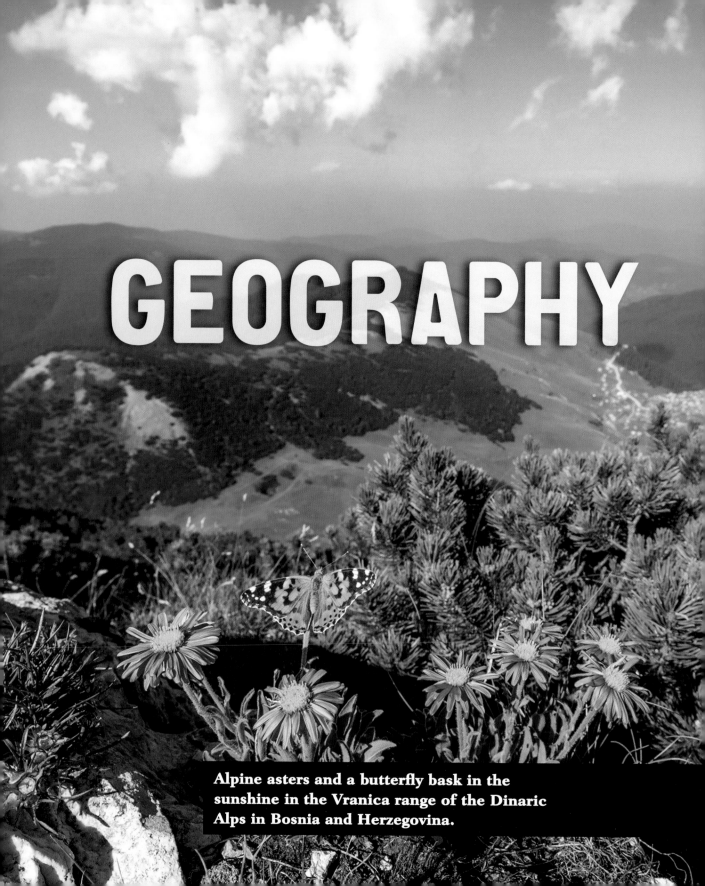

GEOGRAPHY

Alpine asters and a butterfly bask in the sunshine in the Vranica range of the Dinaric Alps in Bosnia and Herzegovina.

BOSNIA AND HERZEGOVINA IS A country in south-central Europe on what is sometimes called the Balkan Peninsula. This landmass is located to the east of Italy and extends eastward to the Black Sea. The region takes its name from the Balkan Mountains of Bulgaria and is an indefinite geographical and political area with borders that vary according to different sources. For the most part, it usually includes the countries of Slovenia, Croatia, Bosnia and Herzegovina, Montenegro, Serbia, Albania, Kosovo (a disputed territory that has proclaimed independence from Serbia), North Macedonia, and Bulgaria. Some sources include the nations of Romania and Moldova to the north, and Greece and a small part of Turkey to the south.

The Balkan region is a place where "East meets West"—where the religions and cultures of Europe collide with those of Western Asia and

Bosnia and Herzegovina is sometimes called "the heart-shaped land" because of its shape on a map, which some see as resembling a heart. Other descriptions say the country is somewhat triangular in shape.

the former Ottoman Empire. Christianity meets Islam here, and within Christianity itself, the Roman Catholic Church and Protestant denominations encounter the Eastern Orthodox faith. In this part of the world, even alphabets bump up against each other. The Cyrillic alphabet of the East butts up against the Latin alphabet of the West. These cultural frictions have contributed to much of Bosnia and Herzegovina's history and identity.

Bosnia and Herzegovina is one country, but the name comes from its two main regions, which have a very vaguely defined border between them. Bosnia occupies the northern areas, making up about four-fifths of the entire country, while Herzegovina occupies a smaller section in the south. (The political divisions of the country are more complicated and are drawn along ethnic lines, including the Federation of Bosnia and Herzegovnia and the Republika Srpska—which literally means "Serb Republic," but it is not the Republic of Serbia, a separate country.)

Bosnia takes its name from the Bosna River; Herzegovina derives from the German word *herzog*, meaning "duke," and the ending *-ovina*, meaning "land." Therefore, the region's name essentially means "dukedom." Bosnia and Herzegovina is a bit of a mouthful in any language, so the name is often shortened for the sake of practicality. There are several ways to do so in English. It's commonly referred to simply as Bosnia. It can also be abbreviated BiH or B&H. In this book, the abbreviation BiH—or just Bosnia—will refer to the entire country unless otherwise stated. (Confusingly enough, the internal political section known as the Federation of Bosnia and Herzegovina—which is not the nation as a whole—is often abbreviated as FBiH or referred to by the shortened name of Federation of BiH.)

This map of Bosnia and Herzegovina shows the country's three internal political entities, including the small Brcko District (*striped*).

THE KARST LANDSCAPE

Terrains of limestone outcroppings, known as karst regions, are found in other parts of Europe as well as in Asia and parts of the United States, but the name was first used to describe parts of Bosnia and Herzegovina, as well as Slovenia. Large areas of these plateaus have deep faults, or cracks, and jagged ravines. These ravines form as rain dissolves softer portions of the limestone, leading to the creation of countless caves and underground streams. When the ceiling of a cave is close to the surface, it may collapse, forming a sinkhole.

In parts of Herzegovina, several depressions may join together to form a polje *(POLE-jeh)—a narrow field where enough soft limestone has eroded to produce soil suitable for some crops or for grazing. Streams that overflow*

This diagram shows a cross section of a karst landform, with underground drainage, the dissolution of soluble rocks, an underground lake, a subterranean river, and a karst spring.

their banks in winter and spring deposit additional rich soil. One polje near Mostar is nearly 40 miles (64 kilomters) long and is called Popo Polje, the Priest's Valley, because it was once church-owned.

The so-called rock rivers—streams that gush out of the side of a mountain and then often disappear underground again—are another unusual feature of karst landscapes. The same river may surface then disappear several times. Underground caves are also interconnected in ways that are not visible on the surface. Shepherds report seeing flocks of sheep disappear into a cave and then emerge from another cave some distance away.

With an area of 19,767 square miles (51,197 square kilometers), this rugged country is slightly larger than the US states of Vermont and New Hampshire combined. The mountains of BiH have fostered a spirit of independence while also making it hard for any outside power either to invade or to control pockets of resistance.

The Dinaric Alps form both a physical barrier and a state boundary between Bosnia and Croatia. This gives Croatia control of the Dalmatian coast and leaves BiH almost completely landlocked, with only about a 12-mile (20 km) coastline on the Adriatic Sea. The Dinaric Alps, and smaller ranges extending east from them, are on geological fault lines, which lead to occasional earthquakes.

MOUNTAINS AND RIVER VALLEYS

The mountain ranges that stretch east from the Dinaric Alps include some of the tallest mountains on the Balkan Peninsula. The highest point in the country is Mount Maglic (MAG-leech) at 7,831 feet (2,387 m), straddling the eastern border with Montenegro.

Mount Maglic lies within Sutjeska National Park, the country's oldest park.

Since 1975, the United Nations Educational, Scientific and Cultural Organization (UNESCO) has maintained a list of international landmarks or regions considered to be of "outstanding value" to the people of the world. Such sites embody the common natural and cultural heritage of humanity and therefore deserve particular protection. The organization works with the host country to establish plans for managing and conserving their sites. UNESCO also reports on sites which are in imminent or potential danger of destruction and can offer emergency funds to try to save the property.

The organization is continually assessing new sites for inclusion on the World Heritage List. In order to be selected, a site must be of "outstanding universal value" and meet at least one of ten criteria. These required elements include cultural value—that is, artistic, religious, or historical significance—and natural value, including exceptional beauty, unusual natural phenomena, or scientific importance.

As of January 2020, there were 1,121 sites listed, including 869 cultural, 213 natural, and 39 mixed (cultural and natural) properties in 167 nations. Of those, 53 were listed as "in danger."

In Bosnia and Herzegovina, there are three cultural sites listed. They include the Mehmed Pasa Sokolovic Bridge in Visegrad, in the Republika Srpska, and the Old Bridge Area of the Old City of Mostar, in the Federation of BiH. The third listing is a group site, the Stecci Medieval Tombstone Graveyards, which is made up of 28 locations in four countries: BiH, Croatia, Montenegro, and Serbia.

The Mehmed Pasa Sokolovic Bridge, a historic bridge over the Drina River, is a **UNESCO** World Heritage site.

This scenic view of Mostar includes the famous Stari Most, or "Old Bridge," on the Neretva River.

The mountainous terrain makes transportation difficult, and there are few east—west roads. Over the centuries, Bosnians settled the fertile river valleys, most of them flowing north into the Sava River, a tributary of the Danube that forms much of the northern border with Croatia. North-flowing rivers in Bosnia include the Bosna, Drina, Una, and Vrbas. In the south, the Neretva is the only major river that carves its way through the Dinarics and across Croatia, flowing west to the Adriatic.

The city of Mostar is located on the Neretva River in a fertile area of cypress and fig trees that is like an oasis within the barren karst landscape. The Sava River valley, along with other river valleys, provides most of Bosnia's best farmland. Although these fertile valleys make up less than 15 percent of the land area, they make farming and raising livestock a major part of the country's economy.

The town of Neum is located on Bosnia and Herzegovina's shoreline—in fact, it's the nation's only coastal town. Geographically, the little town extends west like a tiny arm off the main body of the country, reaching through Croatia's Dalmatian coast to touch the Adriatic Sea. This 12-mile (20 km) coastal strip of BiH cuts off the southernmost part of Croatia's shoreline from the rest of Croatia.

This unusual arrangement is the result of a treaty dating to 1699. Although the arrangement has lasted centuries, Croatia is taking no chances with the future. The two countries signed the Neum Agreement in 1996, in which Bosnia granted Croatia unobstructed passage through Neum, but the agreement was never ratified. In addition, when Croatia became a member of the European Union (EU) in 2013, EU border crossing regulations kicked in, requiring more stringent checks upon leaving and then reentering Croatia on both sides of Neum. This, in turn, created a traffic bottleneck in both directions.

In 2018, Croatia began construction of the Peljesac Bridge to circumvent Neum altogether. Upon completion (expected in 2022), it will connect Croatia's territories by spanning the Peljesac Channel between Komarna on the northern mainland and the peninsula of Peljesac, both of which are Croatian territories.

Meanwhile, with a population of less than 5,000 people, the municipality of Neum is made up almost entirely of ethnic Croats. Nevertheless, it is part of BiH and is its sole outlet to the Adriatic. As such, it attracts tourists to its sandy beaches. However, it does not function as a seaport for freight, though there are plans to build such accommodations. Until then, Bosnia must use the Croatian freight port in Ploce.

In May 2014, the worst flooding in 120 years killed at least 24 people in BiH. In 2019, heavy rains made rivers in the north and central parts of Bosnia overflow their banks, causing damage in many riverside cities.

CLIMATE

The jagged Dinaric Alps have a strong influence on Bosnia's climate. The Adriatic Sea, for example, like other coastal waters, has a moderating influence on the climate, usually producing milder winters and cool summers. However, the Dinarics block the influence of the sea's currents, so the currents affect Croatia's Dalmatian coast but not the interior of Bosnia. Differences in atmospheric pressure between the air above the mountains and the air over the Adriatic produce strong winds—including cold *bora*, or *yougo* (YOU-goh), winds that move from north to south. The result is that Bosnia generally has a modified continental climate, with warm summers and cold winters. A Mediterranean climate prevails in the south, where there are sunny, warm summers and mild, rainy winters.

Temperatures and precipitation levels are strongly influenced by the mountains. Mostar, on the Neretva River and near the Adriatic Sea, has an average January temperature of 43 degrees Fahrenheit (6 degrees Celsius), while Banja Luka in the north is much cooler, at 32°F (0°C). Because of the wind patterns, the north receives its heaviest precipitation in the summer, while rainfall in the south is heaviest in autumn and winter.

The best time to observe the beauty of Bosnia and Herzegovina is in the springtime, when most of the country experiences mild conditions. However, areas at higher elevations might still be covered with snow.

FLORA

News reports of the civil war of the 1990s and of the UN peacekeeping force gave Americans daily television images of Bosnia's spectacular mountains, with their dense forests of beech, oak, and pine. The lumber industry and furniture-making are important parts of the country's economy.

BiH has a surprising variety of plant life. One reason for this is that the mountains have protected some plant species from becoming extinct due to human activity and the invasion of other plant types. Some preserved species date from the ice ages, making the fertile valleys of the north a favorite area for scientists studying the evolution of certain rare species. About 20 percent of the plant species are endemic—not found growing wild anywhere else in the world. Botanists are most fascinated by the types of trees, such as the horse chestnut, a tree that is descended from the rich plant life of the Tertiary period, around 65 million years ago.

Several kinds of shrubs that are now common in the gardens and yards of Europe and North America were spread from Western Asia by way of Bosnia. Lilacs, for instance, were introduced by the Ottoman Turks in the 16th century. The shrubs then made their way to Vienna, Austria, and from there to Western Europe.

Wildflowers fill a meadow in a mountainous region southwest of Sarajevo.

The eyeless proteus lives in caves in the Dinaric Alps.

The Asian variety of forsythia followed a similar route. Through careful selection, the shrub and its blossoms in the North American varieties are larger than those in the Balkans.

MEDICINAL PLANTS For centuries, wild plants have been collected in Bosnia and Herzegovina for healing purposes, and scientists are now analyzing them for possible applications in modern medicine. Lungwort, for example, has long been used by rural healers to ease breathing problems, as the name implies; pharmaceutical companies are now using it in asthma medicines.

Similarly, wild plantain, which is a common roadside weed used in folk remedies, has been found useful for some digestive disorders and as a cough remedy. It is unrelated to the banana-like fruit of the same name.

FAUNA

Bosnia's countless limestone caves, particularly in the north, provide habitats for a variety of unusual animals. Cave spiders, crickets, and several kinds of millipedes are fascinating to scientists studying how animals adapt to environmental conditions. An especially interesting species is the proteus, or olm—an almost colorless creature, similar to a salamander, that has lived in the complete darkness of the caves for so long that it has no eyes.

The mountains, forests, lakes, and streams of BiH have drawn hunters and fishers for several centuries. More than one-third of the country's land area is forested, especially on the lower slopes of the hills and mountains. Hunters are drawn by a variety of wild game—wolves, bears, deer, otters, boars, and the goatlike chamois. Animal migrations to more spacious habitats in Romania and Bulgaria have severely reduced the numbers of such animals in Bosnia. Those that remain are still targeted by hunters.

Other wildlife in BiH includes foxes, wolves, badgers, and wildcats, as well as birds of prey, such as eagles, buzzards, hawks, and vultures. A wide variety of birds populate the Balkan region, ranging from tiny warblers and wrens to storks, cranes, herons, and geese. In spite of environmental problems, many glacial lakes and swift mountain streams still provide trout, bass, and many other game fish.

Hutovo Blato Nature Park in southern Herzegovina provides shelter for more than 240 bird species, as well as other small and large animals. The waters of the park are full of eel, carp, and other freshwater fish. This park was once a popular hunting spot. While hunting is still permitted, so-called photo safaris, in which visitors hunt for the best photo opportunities rather than for the animals themselves, are now heavily promoted.

INTERNET LINKS

https://www.cntraveler.com/story/how-bosnia-ended-up-with -just-12-miles-of-coastline
This article explains Bosnia's unusual extension to the Adriatic Sea.

https://www.globalsecurity.org/military/world/europe/ ba-geography.htm
This article provides an overview of the geography of Bosnia and Herzegovina.

HISTORY

An old tower stands as a testament to history in the medieval town of Pocitelj on the banks of the Neretva River.

MANY PREHISTORIC CULTURES lived in the region that would become Bosnia and Herzegovina. Fragments of those ancient times have been pieced together by historians, with the oldest evidence of human life in the Balkan region dating back 44,000 years or more. Those peoples were hunter-gatherers who ranged across Europe and the Middle East for thousands of years, and little is known about them. In what is now Herzegovina, the earliest cave art was discovered in the Badanj Cave near the town of Stolac. The engravings, discovered in 1976, date to sometime between 16,000 and 12,000 BCE.

By around 7000 BCE, and possibly earlier, Neolithic groups had migrated into the Balkan region, probably from the eastern Mediterranean and the Middle East. They brought concepts of crop cultivation and animal domestication, which set the stage for civilization. These little-known people mined copper and later iron, created sophisticated ceramics, and had organized government, religion, and some form of writing.

It's uncertain when the people who came to be known as the Illyrians moved into the western Balkan region. They originated as an Indo-European nomadic culture and evolved over the centuries into a warrior society with a high level of civilization. The Illyrian kingdoms often warred with the neighboring ancient Macedonians to the south, and by the time of Queen Teuta (who reigned from ca. 231–227 BCE), they were raiding Greek colonies on the Dalmatian coast. In 228 BCE, the Illyrians caused so much turmoil that powerful Roman armies moved in. The Romans finally took control in 33 BCE and transformed the western Balkan Peninsula into a province of the Roman Empire called Illyricum.

THE ROMAN EMPIRE

For several hundred years, the province enjoyed great prosperity and served as a major buffer between the Roman Empire and the tribes of northern "barbarian" societies, like the Goths and Huns, who constantly pressured the empire.

This map shows the Roman Empire (*red areas, with Roman place names*) at its greatest extent in 117 CE, at the time of Emperor Trajan.

Illyricum was so important to Rome that many of the emperors of the later era were Illyrians, chosen by their soldiers—including Diocletian (who lived from 245 to 316 CE and reigned from 284 to 305) and Constantine the Great (who ruled from 306 to 337).

By 285 CE, during the reign of Diocletian, the Roman Empire had grown so vast that it was no longer possible to govern all the provinces from the central seat of Rome. (It had also grown unstable after several decades of poor leadership.) Diocletian divided the empire into West and East, with the Eastern Empire becoming known as the Byzantine Empire because its capital was at Byzantium (today's Istanbul in Turkey). The line between the two parts of the empire went right through the western part of the Balkan region, with Illyricum going to the western sector under Rome, and Diocletian himself ruling the eastern part.

The eastern part of the empire thrived, while the western part fell into decline. Over time, the two parts of the Roman Empire developed very different needs, goals, languages, and cultures, which prevented unity. These divisions still influence and define the Balkan region today.

Two of the major forces contributing to the eventual fall of the West were Christianity and the migrations and invasions of peoples from the north, the so-called barbarians. Although Diocletian fought the arrival of Christianity with persecution and repression, the new religion proved to be too great a force. His successor, Constantine the Great, was the first Roman emperor to convert to Christianity, and by 395 CE, Christianity was the official religion of the entire empire. However, the years of transition from the culture of the ancient Roman pagan gods to the very different concepts of Christianity were not smooth, and many conflicts erupted, undermining the stability of the empire.

MIGRATIONS

One of the most powerful forces shaping European history in those centuries was the westward migration of people from Asia. They came across the plains of today's Russia and Poland and spread into every corner of Europe. Dozens of migrating societies—Goths, Visigoths, Huns, Angles, Saxons, Danes, and others—swept into Europe, often conquering and destroying until they, too, settled and adopted more traditionally civilized ways.

During the sixth and seventh centuries, warlike Slavic tribes moved into the Balkans. The groups that settled in what is now Bosnia were South Slavs, the Croats and the Serbs.

In 1054, Christianity itself would break into two branches, resulting in the Roman Catholic Church (in Western Europe) and the Eastern Orthodox Church. Many Serbs converted to the Eastern Orthodox Church, while other Serbs and most Croats remained part of the Roman Catholic Church.

THE KINGDOM OF BOSNIA

The demographic makeup of modern Bosnia and Herzegovina was taking shape. Roman Catholic Croats occupied much of the north, while Serbs in the south were divided—some Catholic and some members of the Eastern Church. Differences in language and writing systems (alphabets) were also introduced.

Geographic lines also became clearer around 900 CE when a new kingdom, called Bosnia, emerged near the source of the Bosna River. However, independence was soon limited when the powerful Kingdom of Hungary tried to control large areas of the Balkans.

From the late 1100s to 1463, the Hungarians appointed viceroys called *bans* (BAHNS) to rule Bosnia on their behalf. In the 14th century, one of the most powerful bans, Stjepan Kotromanic, added the territory of Hum—later renamed Herzegovina—to Bosnia. The two have remained connected ever since.

Under another strong ban, King Tvrtko I, who ruled from 1353 to 1391, Bosnia and Herzegovina—then the most powerful state in the Balkans—enjoyed a brief golden age. Although Kotromanic and Tvrtko technically ruled as Hungarian viceroys, their reigns are considered the greatest period of Bosnia and Herzegovina's early history.

THE OTTOMAN TURKS

At various times from about 900 to 1463, other outside powers tried to take control of Bosnia. The city-state of Venice as well as Serbia and Croatia all competed for control. None managed to conquer the region.

Then, in 1463, another powerful empire moved in—the Ottoman Turks. From their base in Turkey, the Ottoman rulers took control of much of the land once dominated by earlier Muslim empires. Islam, the Muslim religion, had been born in Arabia in the 600s and had quickly spread outward from there, into North Africa and Spain to the west, and western and southern Asia to the east.

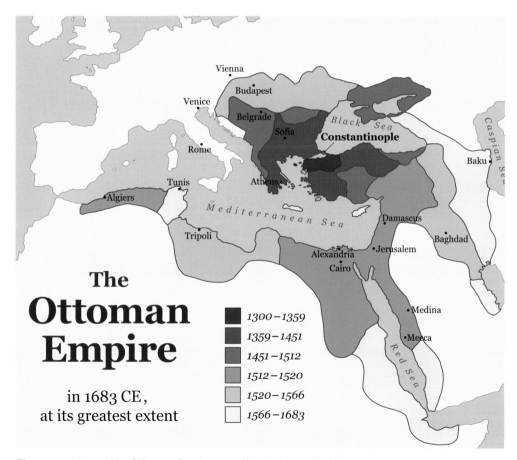

The expansion of the Ottoman Empire over time is shown in this map.

As the Byzantine Empire weakened and collapsed in the early 1400s, the Muslim Ottoman rulers took over much of the area the Byzantines had controlled in southern and eastern Europe. Islam had become one of the world's great religions and had also achieved a high level of civilization, leading the world for several centuries in science, mathematics, architecture, and medicine, with great achievements also in art and literature.

During the 15th and 16th centuries, as the Ottoman Turkish rulers solidified their control over Bosnia and Herzegovina, many Bosnians converted to Islam. With the addition of the Muslim influence, Bosnia now had the ethnic, religious, and cultural mix that still characterizes the country today.

There were now three main groups in Bosnia—groups that are still there today. Bosnian Muslims, also known as Bosniaks, are today the largest group. The second-largest group is the Serbs, who belong to the Eastern Orthodox Church, followed by the Croats, most of whom are Roman Catholic.

NATIONALISM AND WAR

The 18th and 19th centuries were a period of intense nationalism throughout the world. People in a given geographic area who shared a common language, culture, and history longed for nationhood—a nation-state that would allow them to control their own destiny.

This powerful impulse was involved in the creation of the United States in the 18th century and in the independence movements of Latin America, as well as similar movements in Greece, Germany, and Italy a little later. This nationalist spirit rocked the Balkan Peninsula too. After going through frequent wars, plagues, repeated invasions by Austria, and uprisings by the locals, Bosnia and Herzegovina succeeded in breaking away from the Ottoman Empire in 1875 and became a protectorate of the Austro-Hungarian Empire three years later.

By 1900, a larger nationalist movement called Pan-Slavism swept Eastern Europe. This was a desire to unite all Slavic peoples, including the Slavs living in Bosnia, Serbia, Poland, and Russia. The rulers of Austria-Hungary hoped to stall this movement by annexing Bosnia and Herzegovina in 1908.

The United States entered World War I in 1917. The addition of 2 million US troops, plus weapons, food, and other supplies, boosted the Allied Powers, led by Great Britain and France, enabling them to defeat the Central Powers (primarily Germany, Austria-Hungary, and the Ottoman Empire). After leading the United States into the war, President Woodrow Wilson proposed Fourteen Points as the basis for peace. One of the major points was called the right of self-determination—that is, the right of people to choose or create their own nation.

The principle was applied to the former empires, but it was impossible to draw national boundaries that would satisfy every group. Wilson's idea led to the creation of Yugoslavia. However, within the new federation and throughout the Balkans, the spirit of nationalism had not been fully satisfied, and trouble would flare up again.

President Woodrow Wilson is seen here in 1916.

The nationalist drive continued to gain strength, however, especially the desire to create an independent Slavic state limited to the Balkans. It was to be called Yugoslavia—the land of the South Slavs. On June 28, 1914, when the heir to the Austro-Hungarian throne visited Sarajevo, a few Yugoslav nationalists saw a chance to strike a blow for their cause. The royal visitor—Archduke Franz Ferdinand—and his wife, Sophie, were shot dead by a Bosnian Serb named Gavrilo Princip.

The assassination turned out to be one of the momentous events of the 20th century. Austria-Hungary declared war on Serbia, and Russia responded by rushing to the aid of Slavic Serbia. Several interlocking treaties quickly went into effect, and by August 1914, Europe, along with much of the rest of the world, was plunged into the Great War (1914–1918), later called World War I.

Following the horror of the war, the first to feature the use of modern weapons such as airplanes, submarines, tanks, machine guns, and poison gas, the leaders of the victorious Allies redrew the map of Europe in the Treaty of Versailles. Both the Ottoman Empire and the Austro-Hungarian Empire were broken up, and an attempt was made to create new boundaries that would satisfy nationalist ambitions. Bosnia was included in the Kingdom of Serbs, Croats, and Slovenes; in 1929, the name was changed to Yugoslavia.

WORLD WAR II

In 1939, Nazi Germany and other military dictatorships drove the world into war—World War II (1939—1945). Early in the war, Nazi troops marched into Yugoslavia. In the north, they created a puppet government called the Independent State of Croatia, which included Bosnia and Herzegovina. The Germans allowed the Croatian fascist organization, Ustasa, to do as they pleased with the ethnic and religious minorities of Bosnia. The Ustasa killed

An eternal flame burns in Sarajevo to honor the victims of World War II.

an estimated 100,000 Serbs and sent more than 14,000 Jews to gas chambers in the Nazi death camps.

Thousands of Bosnian men and women resisted the Ustasa forces by joining Yugoslav guerrillas in the mountains. The guerrillas, called Partisans, were led by Josip Broz, better known as Marshal Tito. His leadership, combined with supplies from the Allies and the fierce determination of the Partisans, made this the most effective guerrilla force in all of Europe. They forced the Germans out of the country before the war ended in 1945, and Tito was made head of the new government.

Marshal Tito sits at his desk in 1945.

COMMUNIST RULE

Under Tito, Yugoslavia became a communist state and enjoyed 45 years of peace. Postwar Yugoslavia was made up of six republics—Bosnia and Herzegovina, Croatia, Slovenia, Serbia, Macedonia, and Montenegro—plus two autonomous Serbian provinces—Kosovo and Vojvodina. Although Tito enjoyed friendly relations with the Soviet Union, he managed to keep Yugoslavia out of Soviet control. In spite of heavy pressure from Moscow, Tito managed to steer an independent course, while most other communist countries fell under the control of the Soviet Union. In the 1980s, the weaknesses of communism were becoming apparent in the growing economic stagnation. This led to a resurgence of nationalistic spirits. Tito's death in 1980 removed the one person who might have held the federation together. By the late 1980s, the communist structures throughout Europe were beginning to break apart, including the Soviet Union and Yugoslavia.

THE CIVIL WAR YEARS

The breakup of the communist regime in Yugoslavia began in 1991, when Croatia, Slovenia, and Macedonia all declared their independence. The Serb-dominated Yugoslav army—the Armed Forces of Yugoslavia—immediately moved in to crush the independence movements. When Bosnia declared its independence in March of the following year, Serbs in Bosnia and Herzegovina

Communism is a political, social, and economic philosophy in which all property is publicly owned and each person works and is paid (by the government) according to their abilities and needs, as determined by the government. This doctrine is the opposite of liberal democracy and capitalism.

TITO: DICTATOR OF UNITY

From 1945 until his death in 1980, the man known to the world as Marshal Tito ruled the six federated republics of Yugoslavia with an iron hand. As long as Tito was in power, a tight lid was kept on the bitter ethnic and religious feuds that had been seething for decades.

He was born Josip Broz on May 7, 1892, the 7th of 15 children born to a poor peasant family in Croatia. He became a mechanic, worked in Austria, and fought in the Austrian army in World War I. He was wounded, captured by the Russians, and sent to a prisoner-of-war camp, where he learned about communism. After the war, he became active in the Communist Party of Yugoslavia (KPJ), although the government was trying to suppress all communist organizations. Broz was sentenced to five years in prison for his communist activities, and in 1934, he began working underground, adopting the alias of Tito.

In 1941, when German troops invaded Yugoslavia, Tito organized the communist Partisan resistance movement. Although the Allies, including the United States, were reluctant to cooperate with a communist movement, they soon realized that Tito led the most effective resistance forces, not only in Yugoslavia but anywhere in Europe. Finally furnished with weapons and supplies, Tito's Partisans kept Nazi armies at bay, although Tito was seriously wounded and nearly captured twice in surprise raids.

As World War II drew to a close in 1945, Tito consolidated his power. He ignored the Yugoslav government-in-exile in England and simply took control. He abolished the monarchy and made the Federal Republic of Yugoslavia a one-party state. Throughout the years of the Cold War, he refused to surrender any control to the Soviet Union, nor would he cooperate with Western democracies like the United States. Instead, Tito steered an independent course.

Within Yugoslavia, Tito's word was law. In 1953, he was named president of Yugoslavia as well as prime minister, and in 1974, he became president for life. The personal qualities that enabled Tito to remain in power so long included his immense stamina, an ability to adapt to changing conditions, and decisiveness once he chose a direction. He was also an excellent pianist and was said to be one of Europe's best-dressed leaders. However, he was also a dictator—a ruler who kept all power for himself and kept his people under tight control.

The importance of Tito's dictatorship became clear in the years following his death in 1980. Communist control of the country weakened, and the long-suppressed ethnic rivalries and hatreds soon came to the surface, splintering the country and leading to civil war.

saw a chance to take control of the country; they formed an army—the Army of Republika Srpska—and asked the Yugoslav army for help.

Yugoslavia, or what was left of it (primarily Serbia), was happy to assist. Yugoslavian president Slobodan Milosevic was driven by a desire to create a "Greater Serbia" for all ethnic Serbs. This vision compelled him to war against his neighbors—Slovenia, Croatia, Bosnia, and the Albanians of Kosovo—at various stages in the breakup of Yugoslavia. His ruthless and virulent nationalism led to years of bloodshed, took hundreds of thousands of lives, and earned him the epithet "the Butcher of the Balkans."

In addition, many Croats feared that they would be dominated in a Muslim-controlled Bosnia, and they joined in the fighting against the Bosniaks, making it a three-sided civil war.

The war was ugly, bloody, and bitter. The generations of peace that had existed between the different religious groups were buried beneath an avalanche of violence. The Bosnian Serbs, supported by the Yugoslav army,

This wall of names is part of the Srebrenica-Potocari Memorial and Cemetery for the Victims of the 1995 Genocide, which marks one of the darkest episodes of the war in Bosnia.

One of the worst failures of UN peacekeeping interventions in the Bosnian War occurred in the small mountain town of Srebrenica, in the Republika Srpska part of Bosnia near its border with Serbia. The UN had, in 1993, declared the Muslim-dominated town to be a UN "Safe Area"—a humanitarian corridor to be "free from any armed attack or any other hostile act." As such, the town attracted thousands of people from the surrounding region

The Srebrenica-Potocari Memorial and Cemetery for the Victims of the 1995 Genocide opened in 2003. Gravestones in the background mark the remains of 6,643 victims (as of 2019) who have been found, identified, and buried. The victim identification process is ongoing.

who sought safety, and the population of the UN camp there swelled. Despite the presence of the UN, forces of the Bosnian Serb army attacked the town in July 1995. They rounded up around 8,000 Bosniak men and boys and, over the course of a few days, killed them all. It was the worst atrocity in Europe since World War II.

The massacre was carried out under the command of General Ratko Mladic and Major General Radislav Krstic of the Bosnian Serb army. Both would later be convicted of war crimes by the International Criminal Tribunal for the Former Yugoslavia in The Hague, Netherlands.

The UN had left the town under the protection of a peacekeeping battalion of 370 Dutch soldiers. The lightly armed Dutch contingent, however, was incapable of defending the town and did nothing to intervene in the massacre. Later, the Netherlands would be found 30 percent responsible for the deaths at Srebrenica. In 2019, that liability was reduced to 10 percent.

surrounded the once-vibrant capital of Sarajevo and began pounding it with artillery and rocket fire, slowly reducing it to rubble simply because it was primarily a Muslim city. More than 10,000 Sarajevans were killed by artillery and sniper fire, and more than 50,000 were wounded.

The Serbs attacked other Muslim cities and towns, crowding thousands into concentration camps and burying thousands more in mass graves. These murders and atrocities were known as the policy of ethnic cleansing—an effort to destroy or drive away all non-Serbs, much like Adolf Hitler's policy of genocide against Jews before and during World War II. For years after the Balkan conflict, mass graves continued to be discovered, including one in September 2003 that contained around 500 bodies.

At the start of the civil war, Croat forces took part in the attacks on Bosniaks, but they soon found that the Serbs were just as willing to kill Croats as Muslims. Consequently, in 1994, the Croats agreed to a cease-fire with the Bosniaks and joined forces with the Bosnian army. At the same time, as news of the Serbs' ethnic cleansing spread, world opinion condemned the atrocities, and the United Nations (UN) launched an investigation into possible war crimes. The UN also sent in peacekeeping forces, but they had little success at first.

NATO INTERVENTION

Following the Srebrenica Massacre, NATO launched a bombing campaign—led by American and British jets—against the Bosnian Serbs in August 1995. That, along with pressure from the Bosniak-Croat alliance, convinced the Bosnian Serb leaders to lift the siege in Sarajevo and agree to truce talks.

THE DAYTON ACCORDS

At the invitation of US president Bill Clinton, negotiations were held in Dayton, Ohio, in November 1995, producing an agreement that was signed in Paris on December 14, 1995. The Dayton Accords provided for a Serb-controlled republic and a Bosniak-Muslim federation within the nation of Bosnia and Herzegovina. These political divisions, Republika Srpska and the Federation of Bosnia and Herzegovina, remain the two main components of the country

The North Atlantic Treaty Organization, or NATO, is a mutual defense alliance of 29 member countries from North America and Europe. Formed in 1949 in opposition to communism and the Soviet Union, it has since expanded to include several formerly communist nations, including (as of 2020) several countries of the former Yugoslavia: Croatia, Montenegro, and Slovenia.

In 1993, the UN International Criminal Tribunal for the Former Yugoslavia was formed to investigate accusations of war crimes committed by Bosnian Serbs and Yugoslav Serbs in their policy of ethnic cleansing. It took time to identify those involved and then to have them arrested or to persuade them to give themselves up.

Major General Radislav Krstic was among the highest-ranking officers to be put on trial, and on August 2, 2001, he was found guilty for his part in the massacre at Srebrenica. He was sentenced to 46 years in prison, later reduced on a technicality to 33 years.

The president of Yugoslavia, Slobodan Milosevic, was also indicted for his role in ordering the genocide. On March 11, 2006, while imprisoned in The Hague, Netherlands, Milosevic was found dead in his cell. Since 2002, he had been standing trial for war crimes—representing himself—and the trial was thought to be nearing its end. Since he died before it was over, a judgment was never issued; he was therefore never found guilty of the charges brought against him.

The president of Republika Srpska during the Bosnian War, Radovan Karadzic, was also charged, but he went into hiding. He was a fugitive from justice until 2008, when he was found living under an alias in Belgrade, Serbia. He was arrested, tried in The Hague on 11 counts of war crimes, convicted in 2016 on 10 of the 11 counts, and sentenced to 40 years in prison. He appealed the verdict. In 2019, his appeal was not only rejected, but his sentence was also increased to life in prison. Karadzic is still hailed as a hero by many Serbs.

General Ratko Mladic, nicknamed the "Butcher of Bosnia," also evaded capture for many years. Sheltered by Serbian and Bosnian Serb forces and family, he remained at large until his arrest in Serbia in 2011. By then, Serbia was motivated to hand over Mladic; his capture was one of the conditions for Serbia being awarded candidate status for European Union membership. In 2017, Mladic was sentenced to life in prison.

In all, the tribunal prosecuted 161 individuals, including dozens of lesser officials and camp guards, and called 4,650 witnesses. The tribunal completed its mandate in 2017.

called Bosnia and Herzegovina today. Sarajevo, physically located within the Federation of Bosnia and Herzegovina, is the capital of both the country and its smaller entity, the federation of the same name. Sarajevo also functions as the national capital of Republika Srpska, but the administrative center of the entity itself is Banja Luka.

The primary aim of the Dayton Accords was to stop the war, which it accomplished. However, the agreement was only meant to be a temporary measure while a long-term plan was developed. While the tenuous peace has held for more than 25 years, the status quo in Bosnia and Herzegovina isn't without deep tensions to this day. Neither of the two main entities can be said to be satisfied with the arrangement.

INTERNET LINKS

https://www.bbc.com/news/world-europe-17212376
This BBC News timeline lists key events in the history of Bosnia and Herzegovina from 1908.

https://www.icty.org/en
The website of the UN International Criminal Tribunal for the Former Yugoslavia has a wealth of information about its work, including a video documentary about the Srebrenica Massacre.

https://www.lonelyplanet.com/bosnia-hercegovina/background/history/a/nar/8e68f6f5-e1c4-46f8-83c9-1a8d44e8f00d/358721
This travel site offers a good overview of BiH history.

https://www.pbs.org/wgbh/frontline/article/on-the-24th-anniversary-of-the-srebrenica-massacre-bosnian-muslims-continue-to-bury-their-dead
This PBS web page accompanies the *Frontline* program about the trial of Ratko Mladic that aired in 2019.

GOVERNMENT

The blue-and-yellow flags of Bosnia and Herzegovina fly outside a government building in Sarajevo.

SOME OBSERVERS SAY THAT BOSNIA and Herzegovina has the world's most complicated system of government. That's because the structure of the nation itself is complex—essentially it's two countries in one—and how much longer it can last in its present form is anyone's guess.

This arrangement is a direct result of the 1995 Dayton Accords that ended the war in Bosnia. The General Framework Agreement for Peace in Bosnia and Herzegovina, as the agreement is formally titled, established a single sovereign state composed of two parts: the largely Serb-populated Republika Srpska, and the mostly Croat-Bosniak-populated Federation of Bosnia and Herzegovina.

INTERNATIONAL SUPERVISION

In the immediate aftermath of the war, the international community supervised the nation's compliance with the accords. The UN supported sending in a NATO force to enforce the Dayton provisions. This Implementation Force (IFOR) was changed to the Stabilization Force (SFOR) in 1996, after the fighting stopped. SFOR was made up of soldiers from 18 NATO nations, including the United States, and 16 non-NATO countries.

Another agency—the Organization for Security and Co-operation in Europe (OSCE)—was sent in to supervise elections and to maintain a

Signing the Dayton Accords are (*left to right*): Serbian president Slobodan Milosevic, Croatian president Franjo Tudjman, and Bosnian president Alija Izetbegovic. Other world leaders look on as witnesses, including US president Bill Clinton (*behind Milosevic*).

balance among ethnic groups. Other international agencies were involved in governing the war-damaged country. The UN provided an International Police Task Force to train new police forces and to help identify and arrest those suspected of committing war crimes. In addition, the UN, the United States, and the European Union sent money, supplies, and aid workers to assist the war's victims, including more than 2 million refugees.

Overseeing all of this was the Peace Implementation Council (PIC). This international body, made up of representatives from 55 countries and agencies, was established to make sure the peace agreement worked. As of 2020, PIC is still doing exactly that. According to the Dayton Accords, this international control over BiH is to last until the country is deemed politically and democratically stable and self-sustainable. Many in BiH now think of the oversight as meddlesome and unnecessary.

The Office of the High Representative for Bosnia and Herzegovina (OHR), a position created by the Dayton Accords, was given broad powers to ensure civilian compliance with the plan. Essentially, the OHR oversees the country's political process. The high representative is appointed by the 55 countries and organizations that make up the Peace Implementation Council (PIC), the international body charged with implementing the Dayton Accords. As of 2020, the high representative was an Austrian, Valentin Inzko,

The high representative for Bosnia and Herzegovina, Valentin Inzko, speaks during an interview in Sarajevo on December 19, 2019.

appointed in 2009. He was the longest-serving high representative. Many in Bosnia hope that he will be the last.

The high representative is the highest political authority in the country, higher even than the president or prime minister. He or she has the power to remove BiH government officials, including court justices, local government members, members of parliament, and others, if they are deemed to be working against the parameters of the Dayton Accords. And indeed, over the years, the high representative has done just that, getting rid of 192 government officials.

THE NATIONAL GOVERNMENT

The country today is divided into two semi-independent political regions called entities—the Republika Srpska controls about 49 percent of the territory, and the Federation of Bosnia and Herzegovina has 51 percent. In addition, there is a third entity, the small Brcko District, which is an ethnically mixed (Bosniak, Croat, and Serb) administrative unit on the country's northeast border with Croatia.

Since 2008, Bosnia and Herzegovina has been seeking to join NATO, a mutual defense alliance of 29 member countries from North America and Europe. Formed after World War II, its purpose is to safeguard the freedom and security of its members through both political and military measures. The idea is that a crisis in any one country destabilizes an entire area, and, potentially, all of the Euro-Atlantic region.

Marina Pendes, the BiH defense minister (*left*), and General Petr Pavel, the chairman of the NATO Military Committee (*in red cap*), review the honor guards during the welcoming ceremony before their meeting in Sarajevo on November 14, 2017.

Because of NATO, therefore, no single member country is forced to rely solely on its own abilities when facing threats to its security.

However, before being invited to join the alliance, a country has to meet certain conditions. So far, Bosnia has not completely done so. This is largely due to the significant differences in attitude toward NATO in the Federation of BiH and the Republika Srpska. A 2009 poll revealed that while 89 percent in the Federation supported NATO membership, only 44 percent in the RS did. The main sticking point has been the requirement that military facilities be transferred from local (entity) control to state (national) control. The Federation did so with its properties, but the RS has refused.

The pro-Russian Bosnian Serb leader, Milorad Dodik, who in 2018 became one of the country's three presidents, insists that he will block any moves by Bosnia to join NATO. Like the Republika's neighbor Serbia, Dodik insists on military neutrality.

In 2018, NATO approved a Membership Action Plan for Bosnia. The plan is a program of advice, assistance, and practical support for the country. Whether Bosnia chooses to move forward with the plan will depend on the cooperation of Dodik and the Republika Srpska.

The Federation of BiH is divided into 10 subdivisions called cantons, which are further administratively divided into 79 municipalities. These cantons operate as local autonomous units of the Federation. Each canton has its own government, which includes cantonal ministries and agencies. The Republika Srpska has a centralized government and is divided directly into 62 municipalities.

Both the RS and the FBiH govern their own affairs, but matters concerning the entire country are the responsibility of a third, national level of government. While the RS and the FBiH each has its own parliament and president, the BiH nation has a joint presidency divided among the three ethnicities—one Serb, chosen from the Republika, plus one Bosniak and one Croat, chosen from the Federation. The three presidents rotate in and out of office every

Sarajevo's City Hall stands newly reconstructed in 2015 after being destroyed in the war.

On the banks of the Sava River, in the northeast of Bosnia and Herzegovina, lies the municipality of Brcko. Across the river from the city is Croatia. The city and its surrounding area make up the Brcko District, a unique region in the whole of BiH. It's unique not because of any geographical differences, but due to its political status and its ethnically mixed population of about 83,500 people, as recorded in the last census.

The region sits at the junction of the two parts of Republika Srpska, and also borders a point of the Federation of BiH. During the war in the early 1990s, mostly Bosniak people lived there, but since this particular chunk of land stood in the way of connecting the two large sections of Serb-held territory, the Serbs were determined to claim it. To that end, Serb forces stormed the city, driving out the Bosniaks or imprisoning them in camps.

The map shows the Brcko District in dark gray.

When peace talks brought about the end of the war, Brcko was a sticking point that could not be solved. Both sides, the Serbs and the Bosniak/Croats, claimed it. At Dayton, the matter of Brcko had to be set aside while the rest of the accords were worked out. Later, in 1999, Brcko was designated as a special independent, self-governing district, technically owned by both the Republika Srpska and the FBiH, but in essence owned by neither. The district was at first administered by a deputy of the Office of the High Representative, but that supervision effectively ended in 2012.

Today, Brcko has its own constitution and elects its own government. It has its own courts, police, education system, and health services separate from the other entities of BiH. While Brcko's success showcases the potential of a multiethnic society free of Bosnia's historic ethnic hatreds, troubling signs of growing ethnic divisions may yet undermine the entire experiment.

eight months of their four-year term, sharing the position. These presidents are elected by simple majority popular vote. The Republika votes for the Serb position; the FBiH votes for the Croat and Bosniak positions. The presidents are mainly responsible for international affairs. The next election is to be held in October 2022.

The national parliament (Skupstina) consists of two houses: the House of Representatives (Predstavnicki Dom) and the House of Peoples (Dom Naroda). The House of Representatives has 42 members—28 from the Federation and 14 from the Republika. The House of Peoples has 15 members chosen by the local parliaments and must include 5 Bosniaks, 5 Croats, and 5 Serbs.

The day-to-day administration of the country is in the hands of the Council of Ministers. Each minister heads an administrative department, such as transportation, finance, foreign policy, and trade.

INTERNET LINKS

https://emerging-europe.com/intelligence/its-better-than-another-war-a-beginners-guide-to-bosnian-politics
This site gives an analysis of the government structure in BiH.

https://www.globalsecurity.org/military/world/europe/ba-government.htm
This site provides an explanation of the complicated government arrangement in BiH.

https://www.theguardian.com/cities/2014/may/14/brcko-bosnia-europe-only-free-city
This article profiles the Brcko District.

ECONOMY

Two banknotes from Bosnia and Herzegovina, both 50 convertible mark bills, honor poets. Pictured on the bill in front is Musa Cazim Catic (1878–1915), and behind is Jovan Ducic (1871–1943).

4

THE VERY NATURE OF BOSNIA'S segmented structure impacts its economy. The governments of the entities that make up the country add layers of bureaucracy to trade and business dealings, which discourages private investment. In addition, the country's history complicates its economic growth today.

To begin with, the transition from the communist/socialist economic model of Yugoslavia to a free-market economy created one level of challenge. On top of that, the 43 months of civil war in the 1990s had a devastating impact on the economy, and the legacy of the war continues to be an economic factor even now.

A large informal, or "off-the-books," economy that developed in those war years continues to function to some extent. This "gray market" works around the government, which keeps tax revenues lower than they should be. It also prevents an accurate accounting of the country's economic activity, thereby affecting the validity of official statistics, such as the unemployment rate. People who are officially unemployed but who earn money by working "under the table," so to speak, skew those statistics, making a true economic profile difficult to calculate.

Complicating these issues is an internal disagreement on the path forward. For example, while the nation is officially seeking to join the European Union, the leaders of Republika Srpksa—President Milorad Dodik in particular—adamantly oppose all efforts to that effect. Rather than aligning with Western Europe, these RS officials advocate allying with Russia.

Despite these obstacles, Bosnians have made progress in rebuilding the country and trying to create a modern economy. The economy has grown slowly over the first decades of the 21st century.

OLD PROBLEMS

After the civil war, the Bosnian people struggled to overcome the massive postwar problems of refugees, homelessness, and an unemployment rate of over 30 percent of the labor force.

Even before the war, Bosnia's experience with 45 years of communism had left the country with huge economic difficulties. The regime established by Tito in the late 1940s remained independent of the Soviet Union but suffered from many of the same weaknesses as the Soviet system. The theory of communism, as developed by Karl Marx, was that the state, or government, would manage the economy for a time and then the state mechanism would "wither away." The

Buildings bombed during the Siege of Sarajevo remain in ruins.

trouble was that the state never began to wither away. Instead, it became an enormous, entrenched bureaucracy, self-perpetuating and bound in red tape.

In Yugoslavia, including in Bosnia and Herzegovina, the factories, mines, and distribution businesses were run by workers' councils, with the workers electing representatives to operate each business. The state, in turn, established planning boards, which set production goals for every part of the economy. To win awards for meeting goals and avoid punishment for falling short, managers in every factory, shop, and mining operation quickly learned to accept shoddy raw materials simply to keep production going. Regional inspectors overlooked inferior products because the quantity of goods was what counted to the bureaucracy, not quality.

An old ironworks industrial complex in Zenica shows the failure to meet minimum environmental standards, and the region continues to suffer some of the world's highest levels of air pollution.

ENVIRONMENTAL EFFECTS   The emphasis on building a great industrial economy by extracting more and more natural resources and building more factories was disastrous for the environment. State bureaucrats paid little attention to the shocking increase in the pollution of air, water, and land. Cleanup operations, begun in the late 1990s, will continue well into the 21st century.

Even so, BiH today has the building blocks for a healthy mixed economy. Agriculture, logging, mining, manufacturing, and services are all important contributors to the economy. The bigger question is whether political and ethnic forces will drive the country to break apart. Uncertainty about the country's future has had a dampening effect on the private investment the country so badly needs.

Tourism is an important and growing industry in BiH. In 2019, around 1,990,450 tourists explored the country, with 74.4 percent of them visiting from foreign countries. Growth has been impressive in the 21st century, with more tourists arriving every year. To some extent, this is because tourism dropped precipitously during the war years, so in the postwar years, the country had to rebuild its tourism sector almost from scratch. However, the positive figures also reflect the country's focus on investing in and promoting tourism.

Sightseers get a view of Sarajevo from a gondola going up a mountainside.

BiH received a boost in 2006 when the travel site Lonely Planet named Sarajevo, the country's capital, as the 43rd best city in the world. A few years later, the site named Sarajevo one of the top 10 cities to visit in 2010. In 2013, the World Economic Forum reported in its Travel and Tourism Competitiveness Report that Bosnia was the world's 8th-friendliest nation toward tourists.

Sarajevo is the top tourism destination in the country. The red-roofed city is surrounded by towering, forested mountains. It reflects its "East meets West" heritage in its architecture and culture, and it reveals both long-ago and recent history. The city still bears the scars of its brutal siege in the 1990s, but those grim reminders contrast with vibrant new hotels, restaurants, and shopping centers. Although it is a predominantly Muslim city, it has a secular atmosphere that welcomes all.

Other tourist attractions in BiH include its UNESCO World Heritage sites; the cities of Mostar, Banja Luka, and Neum; various national parks; and Mounts Bjelasnica and Jahorina, sites made famous in the Winter Olympic Games in 1984.

AGRICULTURE AND FORESTRY

The northern two-thirds of Bosnia and Herzegovina has good farmland, especially in the fertile river valleys. Grains are the major crops—wheat and corn, and also fodder crops for cattle, sheep, and pigs. A wide variety of vegetables are grown, and the eastern part of the country is famous for its fruits, particularly plums and figs. Farm families also grow a number of specialized crops, including sugar beets, hemp, sunflowers, and grapes for wine. Through much of the year, open-air markets and bazaars display a colorful array of fruits, vegetables, meats, fish, and cut flowers.

Despite its abundant farmland, however, the country's agricultural sector is producing far below its potential. Most of BiH is made up of small family farms that use outdated and inefficient methods. Rural areas suffer from a lack of physical infrastructure for the transport of goods and have insufficient support organizations, such as rural development centers, local action groups, universities and research institutes, training providers, employers' associations, and chambers of commerce.

In an effort to raise BiH's agricultural sector up to EU standards, the European Commission has supplied financial assistance and strategic plans. Its goals are to improve food quality and food safety while also boosting output, but it's a tough challenge. Cooperation and coordination between policy makers, scientific research institutions, advisers, and producers is limited.

FORESTS Like agriculture, timber has long been an important component of the economy. Forests are an abundant natural resource, covering more than 40 percent of the country—one of the highest rates in Europe. Around 80 percent are public forests, and 20 percent are privately owned. Pine and fir are harvested for board lumber and plywood, while hardwoods, such as walnut and oak, are used for furniture manufacturing.

As in the agriculture sector, the country's forest-based sector needs updating in terms of forest management and wood product manufacturing. It needs improved infrastructure, and it needs to eliminate illegal logging. Related issues of energy and environmental policies play into the needs of this sector, as do insufficient data and information gathering and management.

MINING AND MANUFACTURING

During the communist regime of the Yugoslavian era, industrialization increased rapidly, especially heavy mining and the metal industry. The country has an abundance of coal, iron ore, and bauxite. Aluminum production is an important industry, with the Mostar region in the FBiH known as "aluminum valley," while Zenica, also in the Federation, is a center of steel and iron production. This steel and iron supports an automotive industry that produces parts and components, 90 percent of which are exported.

During the civil war, industrial production was cut by more than 75 percent, and a large share of the labor force was out of work. Rebuilding, with help from the international community, was slow because of the need to restore infrastructure—roads, bridges, electric power lines, transportation systems, and communication networks—as well as to rebuild buildings and to replace machinery. By 2003, output was inching back up to prewar levels, but unemployment remained high.

Another important manufacturing sector is textile production, which has traditionally provided jobs for many women in BiH.

INTERNET LINKS

https://www.nytimes.com/2019/05/20/travel/sarajevo-mostar -muslim-culture.html
This travel report highlights the attractions and war damage in Sarajevo and Mostar.

https://whc.unesco.org/en/statesparties/ba
Bosnia's UNESCO World Heritage sites are listed on this page with links, photographs, and videos.

https://www.worldbank.org/en/country/bosniaandherzegovina
The World Bank offers its assessment of BiH's economy.

ENVIRONMENT

A lush, forested landscape in the Vranica mountain range of the Dinaric Alps is healthy and green.

5

BOSNIA AND HERZEGOVINA FACES many environmental challenges. Like other former communist countries in Eastern Europe and the Balkans, some of these stem from the intense industrialization untaken during the communist era. The destruction of the civil war in the 1990s added to the environmental chaos and prevented the government from trying to resolve some of the worst problems. Economic fallout and the need to rebuild infrastructure after the war meant there was little money to spend on environmental cleanup.

Though the country has taken steps to improve the environment, it's hindered by its multiple levels of government, a dizzying array of regulations with a lack of coordination between them, and insufficient accountability.

THE LEGACY OF COMMUNISM

As soon as Marshal Tito and the Communist Party assumed power after World War II, the government became single-minded in its drive to turn what was then Yugoslavia into an industrialized and urbanized

In December 2019, Sarajevo was the most polluted capital in the world. Bosnia and Herzegovina is often listed among the top countries for deaths caused by air pollution, according to the World Health Organization (WHO).

state. No one paid attention to the impact on the environment. During the 45 years of Communist Party rule that followed, more damage was done to the environment in the region than in all the previous centuries of human activity combined.

Communist Yugoslavia used outdated coal-burning furnaces and antiquated machinery because that was what was immediately available. As the number of factories multiplied, the smog hanging over the cities steadily thickened. Rivers and lakes began to look eerily unhealthy. Water supplies began to taste strange, and there were no government regulations limiting what factories, mines, and communities could dump into rivers and lakes.

Like government leaders in other communist countries, Yugoslav officials insisted that these were minor problems, the price that had to be paid to catch up with the capitalist countries of Western Europe and North America. The officials refused to release figures on pollutants from power plants or reveal what pollutants were being spewed into the air by the new steel mills and factories. Tito's government controlled the media, so the people learned little about the environmental alarms being raised by international environmental groups. Foreign reporters were denied access to Yugoslav facilities.

In spite of official efforts to ignore the problems, evidence suggesting that all of Eastern Europe was facing an environmental catastrophe began to leak out. In neighboring Romania, for example, photographs from the town of Copsa Mica showed that everything in the community of 7,000 was covered with a thick layer of carbon black, a pollutant from tire manufacturing; people could not get their clothing or their skin free of the soot, and even the sheep were black. A report from a steel mill in southern Poland indicating that 80 percent of the workers retired with disabilities pointed to the health dangers posed by the outmoded facilities throughout the region.

The fall of communism across Eastern Europe in the late 1980s and early 1990s, including in Yugoslavia, allowed the new governments to begin assessing the environmental fallout from the 45-year communist experiment. In Bosnia and Herzegovina, those first efforts were interrupted by the civil war.

Today, BiH is working to restore its environmental health. The UN and other international agencies are helping in a variety of ways. Complicating the issue, however, is that responsibility for Bosnia's environmental issues, like so much else, is split between the entities—the Federation of BiH, the Republika Srpska, and the Brcko District. There is little or no national-level oversight. For example, the FBiH planned to start taking cars off the road in 2020 that failed to meet certain emissions standards, while the RS made no such commitment. In addition, a lack of regular and reliable data, unclear government accountability at different levels, and a lack of funding adds to the challenges facing the nation.

AIR POLLUTION

Urban areas in BiH are particularly prone to poor air quality. In Sarajevo, for example, traffic emissions, residential heating, and industrial plants release contaminants into the air. The city's geographical position—being surrounded by mountains—affects air movement and causes heavy fog, especially in the winter. These dense air pockets turn to smog when they mix with the pollutants

Air pollution settles over Sarajevo on a winter day.

In the late 1990s, a UN survey revealed that Bosnia and Herzegovina had less than 1 percent of its land set aside as wildlife sanctuaries or forest reserves, the lowest figure for any country in Europe. Since then, Bosnia has added two new national parks, for a total of four.

SUTJESKA NATIONAL PARK *Established in 1962, Sutjeska is BiH's oldest national park. Located on the border with Montenegro, the park includes BiH's highest peak, Mount Maglic, at 7,831 feet (2,387 m) tall. The park also includes the Perucica Forest Reserve, an EU Natura 2000 Special Area of Conservation. This primeval forest is said to be 20,000 years old and has trees that are centuries old. In some places, the forest is said to be almost impenetrable. Sutjeska is also the site of the 322-foot (98 m) Skakavac Waterfall (right), one of the country's highest. A number of rare and endemic species of both plants and animals live in this park, including the Balkan chamois, a kind of goat-antelope hybrid.*

KOZARA NATIONAL PARK *Marshal Tito himself proclaimed this a protected national forest in 1967. Today, it is Bosnia's smallest national park, covering only 13 square miles (34 sq km). This park in the northwestern part of BiH is a low, forested mountain situated between the Pannonian Plain to the north and the Dinaric Alps in the south. The park offers hiking trails, rock climbing, ski runs, and a special hunting area.*

UNA NATIONAL PARK *This park, added in 2008, lies on the border with Croatia. It is named for the Una River, which flows along its border, featuring waterfalls and white-water rapids. River sports and fishing, along with camping and hiking, are popular in this park. Of the four national parks, this is the only one located in the Federation of BiH. The other three are in the RS.*

DRINA NATIONAL PARK *Designated in 2017, this is the country's newest protected nature area as of 2020. It's located in the mountainous municipality of Srebrenica and runs along the Drina River on the border with Serbia.*

and can sit for prolonged periods. During such times, the particulate matter in the air reaches dangerous concentrations that pose significant health risks to residents.

In 2017, the Bosnian city of Tuzla was rated the second most polluted city in Europe (after Tetovo in North Macedonia). Tuzla is a center of industry and is home to six coal mines and the coal-fired Tuzla Thermal Power Plant, the largest power plant in BiH. Air quality in Tuzla regularly reaches hazardous levels.

According to UNICEF, an agency of the UN, these and numerous other industrial urban areas in both the Federation and the Republika have polluted air on a daily basis.

Solutions are likely to be complicated and costly. For instance, coal-burning power plants produce great amounts of sulfur dioxide, but purchasing and installing scrubbers (devices that trap particles from gaseous emissions to prevent them from entering the atmosphere) and other antipollution devices takes time, special skills, and perhaps more money than most electric companies can afford.

Those power plants, plus pollution from smelting plants and motor vehicle emissions, are the worst contributors to acid rain—precipitation that drops high levels of sulfuric and nitric acids on the environment. In Bosnia and Herzegovina, acid rain has destroyed coniferous forests at low elevations and is thought to be a major contributor to the pollution of some lakes and ponds.

The coal-burning Tuzla Thermal Power Plant is a major source of air pollution. In 2019, the FBiH approved construction of a new thermal power plant in Tuzla, to be funded and built by China.

WATER POLLUTION

Bosnia and Herzegovina is blessed with an abundance of water resources. However, much of this water is far from clean. The nation's water-related infrastructure, such as irrigation systems, wastewater treatment plants, hydroelectric power plants, and storage facilities, was damaged during the war. Much of it remains unusable, inefficient, or below modern standards.

Unhealthy water conditions can be seen in this lake in Stanisici in Republika Srpska.

One of the major sources of Bosnia's water pollution woes is agriculture. The modernization and mechanization of farming, especially in the 20th century, led to a tremendous increase in food production, but the cost has been great. The development of large single-crop fields and the increased use of irrigation required the heavy use of chemical fertilizers and pesticides. These chemicals enter the food chain and also leach into the groundwater, eventually reaching the nearest body of water.

Pollutants, such as nitrates and phosphates, cause a buildup of algae in lakes and ponds. That buildup, in turn, leads to a loss of nutrients, killing the algae; the decomposing algae lower oxygen levels, resulting in the death of fish and other marine life.

Government investigators have found that factories routinely dump heavy metals, chemicals, and untreated sewage into the nation's waterways. Court action to force the offenders to stop or to pay fines has been a slow and cumbersome process.

A lack of sufficient waste management systems and recycling programs leads people to dump trash into the rivers. The Drina River, for example, is clogged with tons of trash near a key hydroelectric power plant, where huge garbage islands float on the surface. Multitudes of plastic bottles, rusting barrels, and even old washing machines pollute the rivers, as well as hillsides and wooded areas that become de facto dumpsites.

INTERNATIONAL HELP

The European Union, the UN, and other international agencies have been working with BiH to try to harmonize its environmental laws, management, programs, and goals. The country's admission to the EU depends on it meeting environmental goals that align with European standards. To that end, the EU is supplying financial assistance and expertise, but political will on Bosnia's part is not entirely forthcoming. Without it, there can be no success.

INTERNET LINKS

**https://www.balcanicaucaso.org/eng/Areas/Bosnia-Herzegovina/
Sarajevo-unbreathable-air-191807**
This 2019 article addresses the air pollution problem in BiH.

**https://www.bloomberg.com/news/features/2019-06-21/pollution
-is-choking-europe-s-poorest-region**
This article provides another look at Bosnia's air and water
pollution problems.

**https://www.theguardian.com/cities/2017/feb/14/arcelor-mittal
-failing-emissions-air-pollution-zenica-bosnia**
This article focuses on air pollution in the steel-producing city
of Zenica.

BOSNIANS

Young women wear traditional Bosnian costumes during an international folk dance festival in Banja Luka.

6

ACCORDING TO THE 1995 DAYTON Accords, the nation of Bosnia and Herzegovina is built upon the principle of balance and equality among its three "constitutive peoples"—Bosniaks, Serbs, and Croats. The 2013 census found the population to be comprised of 50.11 percent Bosniaks, 30.78 percent Serbs, and 15.43 percent Croats. A mere 2.73 percent were categorized as "others."

Those statistics alone don't tell the whole story. For the most part, the three groups are not evenly distributed across the land. Rather, they keep separate in their respective entities. BiH is most definitely not a "melting pot," as the United States has sometimes been called. Around 92 percent of all Bosnian Serbs live in the Republika Srpska, while 91.39 percent of Bosnian Croats and 88.23 percent of Bosniaks live in the Federation of Bosnia and Herzegovina. The autonomous entity of the Brcko District is the most ethnically diverse, made up of 42.36 percent Bosniaks, 20.66 percent Croats, and 34.58 percent Serbs.

These figures will no doubt change somewhat after the next census, which should take place in 2023. It should also be noted that the RS authorities dispute the methodology, and therefore the results, of the 2013 census.

RELIGION, ETHNICITY, AND NATIONALISM

Until BiH exploded into civil war in 1992, the country had survived with sharp ethnic divisions. From the 15th century on, the three main ethnic-religious groups lived side by side more or less peacefully, often sharing the same town or city neighborhood.

The three groups—Bosnian Muslims (Bosniaks), Croats, and Serbs—actually belong to the same racial, or ethnic, group. All are descendants of the South Slavs who migrated into the region in the fifth and sixth centuries CE. The differences among the groups would seem to be based more on religion than on ethnic background. Most Croats are Roman Catholics; Bosnian Serbs belong to the Eastern Orthodox Church; and Bosniaks are followers of Islam. In almost any city, it is not unusual to see the spire of a Catholic church alongside the bell tower of an Orthodox church and the minaret of an Islamic mosque.

In the 20th century, however, the powerful force of nationalism began to create deeper divisions. In 1912 and 1913, two separate Balkan Wars erupted as several groups battled to establish independent nations out of the crumbling Ottoman Empire. Bulgaria, Serbia, Montenegro, and Macedonia were involved in these struggles against the Ottomans after Montenegro declared war against Turkey on October 8, 1912. The countries fought against each other in 1913 over the division of Macedonia among the victors. In the 1980s and 1990s, nationalism surfaced again as communist Yugoslavia began to break apart. It was during these years that nationalism came to be associated with religion.

ETHNIC CLEANSING

Bosnian Serbs wanted a strong, independent Serbia. To them, that meant getting rid of the two non-Serb groups—Muslim Bosniaks and Catholic Croats. The Croats, in turn, hoped to be part of an expanded, independent Croatia. The Bosnian Muslims were seen as a stumbling block to the nationalistic aspirations of both groups.

Religious differences that had been tolerated for so long were now seen as symbols of the "enemy"—a source of fear and hatred. When the fighting began,

Serb troops not only attacked Muslim people but also ruthlessly destroyed mosques, bazaars, cemeteries, and other buildings associated with Islam.

The people of Bosnia and Herzegovina had first experienced ethnic cleansing, or genocide, during World War II, when the Ustasa dragged thousands of Serbs, Jews, and Roma (an ethnic group made up of people who were traditionally migrants) from their homes. Many were taken to remote forests and executed; others were shipped to Nazi death camps.

During the Bosnian civil war, Bosnian Serbs, with help from the largely Serb Yugoslav army, made a determined bid to destroy or drive out the country's Muslim population. NATO forces first tried to stop the mass killings by establishing a series of safe zones, where Muslim refugees could escape the Serb death squads.

In July 1995, however, the Serbs attacked the safe area of Srebrenica, which is a town in the eastern part of Bosnia and Herzegovina. These atrocities led NATO to step up its military intervention and the UN War Crimes Tribunal to take more vigorous action.

In Ahmici, a village in central Bosnia, a monument stands to the Bosniak victims of a massacre in April 1993 perpetrated by Bosnian Croats.

DESTROYING TOLERANCE

The war bred hatred and left a legacy of bitterness. It was also costly in terms of the numbers killed—an estimated 7.4 percent of the prewar Muslim population and about 7.1 percent of the Serbian population were lost; Croat casualties were somewhat lower.

THE CROATS IN MOSTAR   For the first two years of the war, Bosnia's Muslims were under attack from both Serb forces and Croats. Between 1992 and 1994, well-equipped Croat troops attacked a number of towns that had large numbers of Bosniaks. Mostar, the country's second-largest city, was besieged much the way Sarajevo was, only in this case by Croats. The Croats hoped to make the city their capital, but their artillery destroyed the Catholic church, a 19th-century Orthodox church, and scores of Islamic mosques. More than 2,000 people were killed during this siege, thousands fled, and more than 5,000 buildings were destroyed.

During that time, most Serb residents fled the city, so today they make up only about 4 percent of the population. Otherwise, Croats and Bosniaks share the city, with Croats slightly outnumbering the Bosniaks.

Mostar has come back to life in the postwar years and is an important tourist destination. However, for the most part, Croats remain on the western side of the Neretva River and Bosniaks on the eastern side, except for a narrow strip on the Croat side. The people of each group tend to regard the other with caution, sometimes with suspicion or fear.

TWO SPECIAL MINORITIES

Two small minorities continue to exist in Bosnia and Herzegovina in spite of heavy persecution.

JEWS   Jews migrated into the Balkan region at several different times, the first as early as the fifth century CE. This first migration was a result of differences between Jews and Christians. Jews had rejected Christianity, and Christians, as a result, had regarded Jews as a foreign people. Perhaps the largest

THE NEW "OLD BRIDGE"

For many centuries, a magnificent bridge with a gleaming white arch spanned the Neretva River at Mostar. The bridge, called Stari Most—Turkish for "old bridge"—was built by the Ottoman Turks in the 16th century. According to legend, the arch covered such a large span that the great Turkish ruler Suleiman the Magnificent ordered that the builder, architect Mimar Hajrudin, be executed if the arch collapsed. Hajrudin fled just before the scaffolding was removed. He could have remained. The bridge, between two jagged bluffs, remained solid for four centuries.

Over many generations, Stari Most became a symbol of unity between the Muslims on the eastern side of the bridge and the Croats on the western side. It was also known for the displays of high diving by daredevils who plunged

A man jumps from Stari Most while onlookers cheer.

65 feet (20 m) into the churning waters of the Neretva.

When the civil war began, the bridge was badly damaged by artillery fire. Then, in November 1993, Bosnian Croats provoked outrage by shelling the damaged arch again and again, until it crashed into the river.

The project of rebuilding the bridge became a new symbol—a symbol of the effort to reconcile a community and nation that was now bitterly divided. As early as 1996, Austria provided funds and Turkey sent engineers skilled in building with limestone. In August 2003, the Muslim mayor of Mostar and his deputy, a Croat, helped use a crane to lift a gigantic keystone into place in the middle of the 89-foot (27 m) span. In 2005, the Old Bridge Area of the Old City of Mostar was added to the UNESCO World Heritage List. The listing states, "The reconstructed Old Bridge and Old City of Mostar is a symbol of reconciliation, international co-operation and of the coexistence of diverse cultural, ethnic and religious communities."

A door of an abandoned, ruined synagogue in Mostar is still adorned with the symbols of Judaism.

numbers came during the Spanish Inquisition in 1492, when 160,000 Jews were expelled from Spain after King Ferdinand and Queen Isabella I issued an edict against them. Other Jews came in the 19th and 20th centuries to escape persecution in Poland and Russia. While forced to live in separate sections of cities called ghettos in most of Europe, Jews found a more friendly reception in Muslim areas. Most Bosnian Jews were city dwellers, with a large percentage being professionals, including teachers and physicians. They added important dimensions to the culture of Bosnia and Herzegovina.

From 1933 to 1945, during Adolf Hitler's vicious campaign to destroy the Jews of Europe, an estimated 6 million Jews were killed in Nazi concentration camps scattered throughout southern and eastern Europe. A few thousand returned to cities like Sarajevo and Mostar, but the numbers have remained small. There is a Jewish museum in Sarajevo and a synagogue, but in most of Bosnia, empty synagogues and untended cemeteries are stark reminders of the once vibrant Jewish culture.

According the World Jewish Congress, there were between 500 and 1,000 Jews living in BiH in 2015. This small community is largely made up of Sephardic Jews, descendants of those who fled the Spanish Inquisition.

ROMA The people formerly known as Gypsies (the name is now considered derogatory) once numbered up to 4 million throughout Europe. They had originally migrated west from northern India in the 11th century CE. They have always been fiercely independent, living a nomadic life and wandering throughout Europe with little regard for national borders. They are known today as Roma. Their language, Romani, is not a written language but has been used by Roma throughout the world. The Romani language, unknown to others, has been useful to Roma as a kind of secret code, but it has also served to make authorities suspicious of them. The world's largest Roma populations have been in Eastern Europe, and as many as 100,000 lived in scattered groups in the hills and mountains of Bosnia and Herzegovina before World War II.

Like Jews, they were victims of Hitler's policy of genocide, and several million died in the death camps.

The Roma traditionally held occupations on the fringes of society—junk dealers, horse traders, circus performers, and fortune-tellers. Their colorful way of life has appealed to novelists and filmmakers, and their music has had a lasting influence, providing melodies for contemporary songwriters and for classical composers such as Franz Liszt. Fewer than 15,000 remain in Bosnia today.

INTERNET LINKS

https://www.haaretz.com/world-news/europe/.premium-why -sarajevo-s-jews-believes-it-s-the-safest-place-in-europe-1.5430455
This article spotlights the tiny Jewish community in Sarajevo.

http://www.sarajevotimes.com/when-to-expect-the-next-census -in-bosnia-herzegovina
This 2020 article provides more information on the past and next census in BiH.

https://whc.unesco.org/en/list/946
The World Heritage listing for the Old Bridge Area of Mostar includes a fascinating video on the bridge's destruction and rebuilding.

LIFESTYLE

A McDonald's is just another restaurant on a busy street in Sarajevo.

7

BOSNIA AND HERZEGOVINA HAS been in a state of transition for more than three decades. For many Bosnians, that's the course of their entire lives. It has been a time of transformation from war to peace, from communism to democracy, and from a centralized economy to a free-market economy.

It has also been a metamorphosis in personal identity. After all, the internal mapping of the nation gained all new boundaries after the war—the Inter-Entity Boundary Line (IEBL)—and people have needed to come to terms with where they fit within those lines. The change has had the effect of hardening personal identity in allegiance with one's ethnic-religious group—Bosniak, Croat, or Serb.

LIFE IN SARAJEVO

Sarajevo is the capital of all of Bosnia and Herzegovina, but it falls within the FBiH. Its former suburb, East Sarajevo (Istocno Sarajevo) is on the other side of the IEBL, in the RS. In postwar Bosnia, it has become a separate Serb city.

During the war, Sarajevo suffered thousands of deaths and intense destruction during the siege from April 5, 1992, to February 29, 1996, by the Serb army. Today, more than two decades later, Sarajevo is again a lively city, bursting with renewed energy. Shops and restaurants line the streets. People stroll along Ferhadija, the main pedestrian thoroughfare,

For years, people in Sarajevo boasted (or lamented) that there was no McDonald's restaurant in the city (or indeed, the entire country). Rumor had it that market research had determined that Sarajevans would never accept the Big Mac over the local favorite, *cevapi*—a type of grilled sausage, but in 2011, the first McDonald's opened with much hoopla on Marshal Tito Street. Another opened there in 2019, and one opened in Mostar— bringing Bosnia's total Golden Arches presence to three.

or sip Bosnian coffee at one of the many outdoor cafés. Foreign visitors have begun to return, too, including thousands who are connected to the many international agencies that have offices in the city. These visitors come from many countries, giving Sarajevo a cosmopolitan feel.

SARAJEVO ROSES Though many parts of the city have been rebuilt, many remaining buildings, bridges, and other structures still show the pockmarks of bullets and bombs. On some streets and sidewalks, craters left by the mortar strikes have been filled with red resin to create small memorials. These bloodlike spray patterns are called "Sarajevo roses," and there are about 200 of them throughout the city. The so-called roses look disconcertingly—but deliberately—like giant bullet wounds and serve as reminders of the siege.

LIFE IN BANJA LUKA

Today, Banja Luka is Bosnia's second-largest city, with around 200,000 people. It lies on the banks of the Vrbas River, in the northwestern part of the Republika Srpska. The city is the entity capital, but it is the de facto national capital for the Bosnian Serbs, with the republic's red, blue, and white flags fluttering from many municipal buildings.

Banja Luka was a fairly multicultural city before the war. During the war years of the 1990s, however, almost all of its Bosniak and Croat population was expelled—around 60,000 people. The Bosnian Serbs tried to further rid their city of Muslim influence by blowing up all 16 mosques. Although most of the mosques have been rebuilt with private donations, most vestiges of Muslim life have disappeared. Street names, school names, and other public places have been changed to reflect only Serb history and culture. Today, the city is about 90 percent Serb/Orthodox Christian.

People sit at an outdoor café on a street in Banja Luka.

With the war behind it, Banja Luka now attracts tourists. It's a peaceful city of cafés, museums, parks, historic cathedrals, monasteries, and other beautiful buildings. The surrounding region is rural and green. The Vrbas River provides kayaking, rafting, and other water sports.

CITY AND COUNTRY

Slightly more than half of Bosnia's population lives in rural areas—mostly small farm villages. As in other societies, rural Bosnians tend to be a little distrustful of outsiders and uneasy about new ideas or ways of doing things. Their farming methods often seem more appropriate to the early 1900s than to the early 2000s. Tastes in everything from clothing styles to music tend to favor tradition.

In spite of their distrust, rural Bosnians are considered warm and friendly, with a strong sense of being hospitable. A favorite time of day is the coffee hour, a time to visit with friends and neighbors. Women will gather in a neighbor's kitchen or yard with cups of coffee and their embroidery. While they talk, they stitch colorful designs on scarves, towels, blouses, and other items.

A shepherd herds a flock of sheep in the early morning in Lukomir. At 4,820 feet (1,469 m), it is Bosnia's highest village.

There is a strong oral tradition in Bosnia and Herzegovina, and every village seems to have at least one gifted storyteller. At any social gathering, such as a birthday party or wedding, the storyteller will entertain with tales about the family, the village, the days of Yugoslavia under Marshal Tito, or some great victory in the recent years of war.

The lifestyle in Bosnia's cities, however, is not markedly different from that in other parts of Europe. Casual clothes are seen more often than business attire. Women wear more conservative clothes than Americans, but dress pants or jeans are common, as are polo shirts and T-shirts. City residents are much more aware of life in other parts of Europe, including the latest films and songs. ATMs are visible, and Wi-Fi is available in most cafés.

FAMILY TIME   People spend a lot of time with their families, and many families take an evening stroll in their neighborhood or in the city center. Nightlife is also popular. Bosnians enjoy dance clubs and jazz clubs, movies, concerts, and cafés, although going out to dinner is not nearly as common as in the United States.

Until the civil war, there was considerable mixing among Bosniaks, Serbs, and Croats. Through people's jobs, friendships, or university study, members of the three groups intermingled freely. Intermarriage became quite common; residential areas and apartment buildings became increasingly multiethnic. The war changed that atmosphere. People are now more clannish, and they cross ethnic-religious boundaries with reluctance.

In addition, members of each group tend to follow the rules of their religion more closely than in the past. Still, many people, on their own or through small organizations, are trying to restore contacts and rebuild a sense of trust. Everyone agrees, though, that years of effort will be required and that Bosnia and Herzegovina may never get back to what was normal in 1991.

WOMEN

In some ways, life under the Yugoslav system opened opportunities for women. Under communism, the government pursued an official policy of equality. Women were encouraged to pursue professional careers long closed to them.

Bosnia has long had a cultural and religious patriarchal tradition according to which women are expected to be submissive to men. Since independence, those social norms and expectations have returned, and the role of women has suffered a setback.

Today, Bosnia has Europe's widest gender pay gap, with women making only 54 percent of what men make. Bosnia has one of Europe's highest unemployment rates, hovering around 20 to 25 percent. In times of high unemployment, women are typically cut out of job opportunities as priority is given to men. However, there's more to it than that.

In urban areas, society tends to be more progressive. Women look to the West and want the same lifestyle. In rural areas, women tend to be less educated and hold more traditional views of gender roles. A lack of childcare facilities, especially in rural areas, generally makes it difficult for most Bosnian women with children to work outside of the home.

In 2003, Bosnia and Herzegovina passed the Gender Equality Law to promote and advance equality between men and women. Laws related to elections, as well as other laws, were also amended. As a result, the election law requires that 30 percent of all candidates must be women. That does not mean that 30 percent of government officials are female. In 2020, at the national level, women made up 13 percent of the House of Peoples and 21 percent of the House of Representatives.

CHILDREN

Although Bosnia has returned to peacetime life, for many people who were children during the war, psychological wounds have not healed. UN officials estimate that more than half the country's children suffered severe trauma from the war and its aftermath. Girls as young as nine were victims of assault. Many children were orphaned, and many more had no homes to return to.

In the postwar years, the UN Children's Fund (UNICEF) and other UN agencies worked with private organizations such as Oxfam and Save the Children to provide medical care and counseling. Every effort was made to locate missing family members and to arrange adoptions for orphans.

In 2017, the War Childhood Museum opened in Sarajevo. The brainchild of Jasminko Halilovic, a Sarajevan "war child" himself, the museum presents the experiences of people who were children during the war in Bosnia. The exhibits—deliberately apolitical—aim to tell the experiences of the war from a child's perspective, through testimonies, photographs, diaries, toys, other objects, and oral history interviews. In 2018, the Council of Europe awarded the new institution its prestigious Museum Prize.

EDUCATION

Rebuilding Bosnia's schools after the war was a mammoth undertaking. Many schools were destroyed, especially in Muslim areas, where they were favored targets of artillery and bombs. As the schools were being rebuilt, the UN Office of the High Representative for Bosnia and Herzegovina created a huge controversy by trying to rid schoolbooks of anything that could be considered inflammatory or hate speech. While the motive was good, carrying out the policy created what some critics said was censorship of art, literature, and music.

In Muslim-controlled regions, the committee struck down everything that seemed even remotely anti-Muslim. Reproductions of works of art with heroic war scenes were removed from textbooks, and so was the Yugoslav national anthem. Critics of this policy argued that Bosnian history was being rewritten to strike out events that might be troublesome to one group or another.

Once the controversy over textbooks started, leaders of ethnic-religious groups decided that each group would use separate textbooks. Thus, Bosniaks learn from "domestic" textbooks, which include Islamic symbols, even on the cover. Croat and Serb children read books that make their ethnic group the heroes of Bosnian history. Many people feel that these trends will simply splinter the society further, and a number of efforts are underway to find a better approach.

Taking a step further, many communities instituted a form of segregated education called the "two schools under one roof" policy. In about 60 schools across the Federation of Bosnia and Herzegovina, the school building is literally

Beginning in 2015, a surge of people from the Middle East, Asia, and Africa began arriving in Europe. The wave of migrants came by foot and by boat across the Mediterranean Sea in record numbers. Many were escaping war, violence, or persecution in countries such as Syria and Afghanistan. Others, mainly from South Sudan or other countries in sub-Saharan Africa, were seeking better economic opportunity. All were desperate. The surge of migrants came to be called the European refugee crisis or migrant crisis. Numbers finally began to slow, but not stop, in 2019.

This image from October 2019, shows refugees and migrants at the Vucjak camp.

Many of the migrants were following the so-called Balkan route, passing through the Balkans while hoping to reach EU member countries like Germany. In 2016, after Hungary built a wall and several other countries, including Croatia, closed their borders to new migrants, Bosnia found itself overwhelmed. In 2019, more than 29,000 migrants arrived in the country, 21 percent more than in 2018. Thousands became stuck in the Bihac region, on the Bosnian side of the Croatian border, unable to go any farther. Most were single men, but there were some women and children, as well as many unaccompanied minors. UN- and Red Cross–run camps and reception centers were overrun. Many of the refugees, coming from warmer places, were not prepared for the frigid winter temperatures in Bosnia.

One camp in particular, the Vucjak refugee camp, attracted international attention for its "dangerous and inhumane" conditions. It had no electricity, sanitary facilities, or potable water. In December 2019, in the face of rising criticism, Bosnia finally dismantled the camp, busing some 800 people to Sarajevo.

The migrants never wanted to remain in Bosnia to begin with, and Bosnia doesn't seem to want them. Even with EU financial assistance, Bosnia has been unable to manage the situation. The Republika Srpska, for its part, refuses to accept any migrants on its territory, but it's not alone. Many other regions in the country have also rejected hosting refugee centers.

separated into a Croat side and a Bosniak side. The separate classrooms use different books and have different curricula. There is no interaction between the Croat and Bosniak schoolchildren.

In recent years, the Organization for Security and Co-operation in Europe (OSCE), which oversees education in Bosnia, has been pushing to eliminate this segregated education system. It warns that "ethnically oriented curricula" impede reconciliation, perpetuate divisions, and "limit economic development and jeopardize the long-term stability and security."

INTERNET LINKS

https://balkanist.net/banja-luka-amnesia
A man who grew up in Banja Luka grimly observes the changes his city has gone through.

https://www.nytimes.com/2019/05/20/travel/sarajevo-mostar -muslim-culture.html
This first-person travelogue presents a particular view of Bosnia.

https://www.opendemocracy.net/en/can-europe-make-it/women -in-bosnia
The gender issue in Bosnia is the focus of this article.

https://www.osce.org/mission-to-bosnia-and-herzegovina/ 404990?download=true
This OSCE report details the problem of segregated schools in Bosnia.

https://www.thenewhumanitarian.org/news-feature/2019/12/24/ migrants-refugees-Bosnia-Croatia-Vucjak-camp
This site provides a look at the problematic migrant situation in Bosnia.

https://www.warchildhood.org
This is the website of the War Childhood Museum.

The Organization for Security and Co-operation in Europe (OSCE) is an intergovernmental organization created in 1975 to address a broad range of concerns relating to security in member states. Among those are human rights, national minorities, education, electoral oversight, conflict prevention, crisis management, and post-conflict rehabilitation. The organization has a special office in Bosnia and Herzegovina to promote stability and reconciliation.

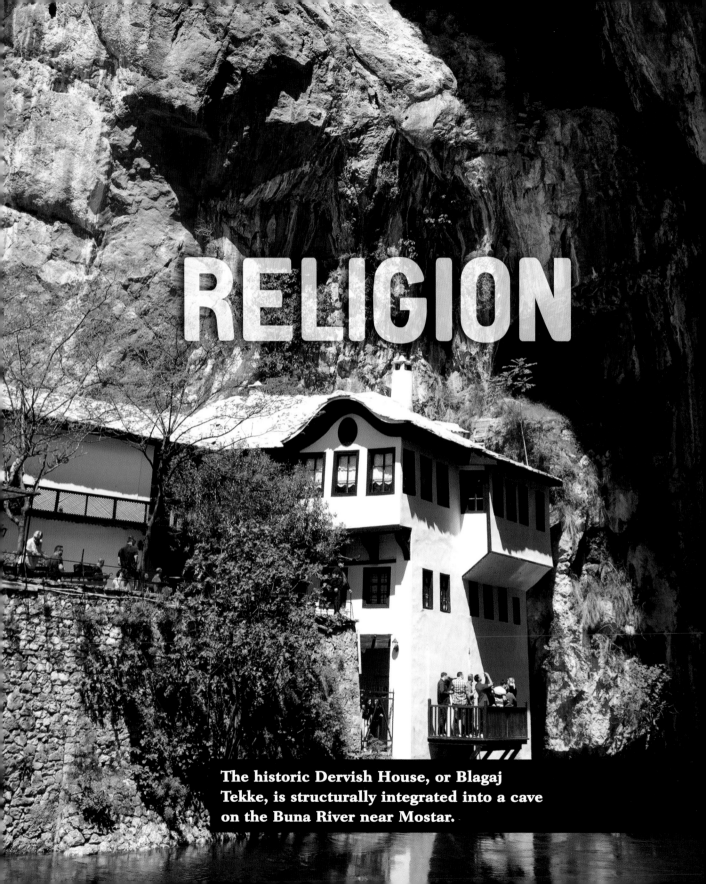

RELIGION

The historic Dervish House, or Blagaj Tekke, is structurally integrated into a cave on the Buna River near Mostar.

8

Y UGOSLAVIA WAS A GREAT MIX OF religious, ethnic, and linguistic groups. In the six constituent republics, Roman Catholics formed the largest group in Croatia and Slovenia; Muslims were a majority in Bosnia and Herzegovina; and the Eastern Orthodox religion was dominant in Serbia, Montenegro, and Macedonia. After Tito's death in 1980, tensions between the groups began to grow. When Yugoslavia began to break apart around 1990, those tensions exploded.

Today, Bosnia is a secular nation. There is no official religion, either nationally or at the entity level. Constitutionally, there is freedom of religion. The nation is divided along ethnic lines—Bosniak, Croat, and Serb. However, since all three groups are basically the same in language and physical appearance, the one difference that stands out is religion.

It may be more accurate to say the nation is divided along ethno-religious lines. The term "ethno-religious" denotes ethnic groups that are unified by a common religion. Bosniaks are Muslim, Croats are Roman Catholic, and Serbs are Eastern Orthodox Christian. The breakdown is approximately 50 percent Muslim/Bosniak, 31 percent Orthodox/Serb, and 15 percent Catholic/Croat. All three groups are South Slavic, and all are Bosnians.

Bosnia's schisms don't appear to be based on spiritual beliefs or the claim that one group's way of worship is superior. In fact, few people seem to be deeply devout. Some observers suggest that the religious differences are little more than labels for deeply felt nationalistic strivings. Essentially, these concerns boil down to one question: Who (or which group) holds the power?

In the early 1990s, as the conflict among the groups escalated, people began to see the other groups' religious practices as unpleasant at first, and eventually as hateful. Once the war started, people fought with great ferocity to destroy the symbols—as well as the people—associated with the hated religions or to defend their own religious community from atrocities committed by "the enemy." As is usual in wartime, no matter which peoples are involved, the "other" is dehumanized as "the enemy," which makes hatred and violence toward them easier to act upon.

The Martyrs' Memorial Cemetery in Sarajevo, for Bosnian soldiers killed in the civil war, also houses the tomb of Alija Izetbegovic, independent BiH's first president.

ISLAM

Islam was founded by the Arab prophet Muhammad in the seventh century CE. The holy book of Islam—the Quran (sometimes written as Koran)—is regarded as "the Word of Allah (God)." Muslims share some beliefs with Jews and Christians, especially the belief in one God. They also accept Old Testament prophets, such as Abraham and Moses, and they think of Jesus as one in a line of those holy prophets, with Muhammad being the last and greatest of them. Muslims believe Muhammad received and wrote down messages from God, as dictated in Arabic by the Archangel Gabriel, that form the central text of the Quran.

Muslims are expected to follow the Five Pillars of Islam: to recite the profession of faith at least once; to observe the five daily calls to collective public prayer; to pay the zakat (purification) tax to support the poor; to fast daily from daybreak to sunset during the holy month of Ramadan; and to

Muslim men pray during the holy month of Ramadan at the Old Town Mosque of Sarajevo.

During the civil war, many Bosnian mosques were damaged or completely destroyed, including the acclaimed Ferhat Pasha Mosque in Banja Luka (right). Often called the Ferhadija Mosque, it was a striking example of Ottoman Islamic architecture, built in the 16th century. In the later part of the 20th century, the mosque was put under UNESCO World Heritage protection; however, that did not stop Serb fighters from destroying it in 1993. Using explosives, the Serbs reduced the beautiful building to rubble.

Ferhat Pasha was one of 16 mosques destroyed in Banja Luka—all demolished with no regard for their architectural or historic value. The devastation was carried out as part of the Serb authorities' ethnic cleansing campaign. Later, after the war, the International Criminal Tribunal for the Former Yugoslavia in The Hague found the Serb leader Radoslav Brdanin guilty of organizing the destruction of Muslim property. He was sentenced to 32 years in prison.

In 2001, when 300 members of the Muslim community gathered to rebuild the historic mosque, around 1,000 Serbs attacked the group with rocks and fire, causing one death, numerous injuries, and much terror. The rebuilding project was called off. Eventually, however, the mosque was rebuilt as authentically as possible and is now listed as a National Monument of Bosnia and Herzegovina. It reopened in 2016.

perform, if they are able to, the hajj (pilgrimage) to the holy city of Mecca in Saudi Arabia at least once in their life.

Muslims everywhere consider themselves members of a single worldwide community. In practice, however, there are differences from country to country, and there are differences between the two main branches of Islam, Sunni and Shia. These two branches don't always get along. A majority of Bosnian Muslims, however, identify as "just Muslims," while about 38 percent claim to be Sunnis.

The Ottoman Turks brought Islam to the Balkan region in the late 15th century. Once in power, they established a policy of tolerance toward other religions. Jews, however, were given special consideration and were often appointed to high administrative posts. Christians, while tolerated, soon learned that they could rise in the government or society only if they converted. There was also a good deal of discrimination. Christians, for instance, could not wear extravagant clothing or the color green (a color associated with Islam). They were taxed more heavily than Muslims, and they could not build new churches without permission. There were also many petty forms of discrimination, such as having to dismount when a Muslim rode by on their horse. As a result, a good number of Christians became Muslims, just to fit in. The remaining Balkan Christians held those converts in particular disdain. Over the many long centuries, these emotions were passed down through the generations and still hold sway today.

A DIFFERENT SORT OF ISLAM Today, compared to many other predominantly Muslim nations, Bosnia is more liberal about religious and cultural matters. Only a minority of Bosniak women wear the Muslim headscarf, or hijab, and the culture is more European than Arab. In Sarajevo, a Muslim-dominated city, there are many restaurants and bars that serve alcohol, which would not be found in more conservative Muslim cities. The capital city also hosts European-style arts festivals featuring jazz, pop, rock, and hip-hop music.

EASTERN ORTHODOXY

About 1,000 years ago, the early Christian Church broke into two main branches: the Roman Catholic Church in the West and the Orthodox Church in the East.

In the centuries that followed, the two churches steadily grew farther apart, especially over the authority of the pope in Rome—the head of the Roman Catholic Church.

Today, the pope in Rome remains the head of the Roman Catholic Church. In the East, the bishop, or patriarch, of Constantinople (today's Istanbul) leads the Eastern Orthodox Church. The patriarch, however, does not have the authority of a pope, and the Orthodox Church itself less centralized. Rather, it is a "communion" of self-governing national churches. In Bosnia and Herzegovina and Serbia, for example, the Serbian Orthodox Church is the primary Orthodox institution. Other branches include the Greek Orthodox and the Russian Orthodox Churches.

As the Orthodox church service evolved, it became very different from the Roman Catholic service. Probably the most notable difference is that the Orthodox service is far more ornate, reaching all the senses through rich colors, elaborate ceremonies, Eastern music, and incense. The Orthodox Church fills its churches with many icons—formal paintings of holy figures. Praying to an icon is considered the same as praying to the person pictured.

The magnificent interior of the Holy Transfiguration Orthodox Cathedral in Trebinje is a typical example of ornate Orthodox church architecture and decoration.

The Serbian Orthodox Church, in common with all Eastern Orthodox churches, places great importance on icons, or holy images.

Icons are flat panel paintings featuring images of holy men and women. They typically incorporate rich colors and gold leaf, and they are illuminated by candles. An icon is regarded as a kind of window between the earthly and the spiritual worlds, a window through which an inhabitant of the celestial world—a saint, or Jesus

Icons glow on the wooden altar of the Cathedral of Christ the Savior in Banja Luka.

Christ himself—looks into the human world. The image recorded in the icon is a sacred one because of the belief that the true features of the heavenly spirit have somehow been imprinted in a two-dimensional way on the icon. The icon is sacred because Jesus Christ or a saint becomes incarnate, or embodied, in the very materials of the icon—the wood, plaster, paint, and oils. The veneration shown to an icon is not worship of the object itself but rather of the divine image as glorified by the object.

As a form of art, icons have no concept of authorship. This is one of the differences between the art of the icon and the art of Western Christianity. For centuries, the craft of producing icons was done in monasteries, with a group of monks working together on one icon. One monk might work on the eyes or hair, while another would devote himself to painting the robes of the figure being represented. Icon painters (iconographers) prepared themselves for painting through fasting, prayer, and Holy Communion because it was believed that to paint Jesus Christ better, one must have a close relationship with God. Today, some iconographers are specially trained laypeople.

Among the most famous icons in Bosnia are those in the Church of the Assumption in the town of Cajnice in the RS. The gold and silver image of the Virgin Mary—the mother of Jesus Christ—is believed to have been painted by the Apostle Luke and is said to have miraculous powers.

At 6 p.m. on June 24, 1981, six Bosnian Croat teenagers were on a hill near the town of Medjugorje, when they were startled by a vision. They said they saw a beautiful young woman holding an infant. Frightened, the young people ran away, but four of them returned the next day with two other friends. The apparition returned, and this pattern was repeated for several days.

Word spread among the hill towns, and crowds began to follow the teens. On the fifth day, the lady spoke, telling the children that she was Mary, the mother of Jesus, and that she was bringing a message of love, urging people to work for peace and to pray to God for peace. An estimated 10,000 people were there that day, but apparently only the original seers could see or hear her. As the appearances continued, however, others said they were able to see her and hear the message. The Catholic Church had the seers examined, and they were found to be in good health—mentally and physically—but church authorities remained reluctant to sanction the appearances as miracles. Skeptics have offered alternate physical and psychological explanations for the phenomenon.

Since 1981, the occurrences at Medjugorje—which is in the Herzegovinian region near the border with Croatia—have continued to fascinate Catholics and non-Catholics from all over the world. The visionaries, now adults, reportedly still see the apparitions, and a few have traveled widely to tell of their experiences.

In 2019, after conducting an official study, the Vatican—the seat of power in the Roman Catholic Church—approved the site for pilgrimages. The move does not mean the Catholic Church has—as yet—authenticated the occurrences of the apparitions. Rather, it is an acknowledgment of the spiritual benefits to those who visit the place. Today, around 1 million people visit the town each year, and a youth festival is held each summer. The town has profited economically from the phenomenon, and a multitude of hotels, churches, shrines, monuments, clergy, and souvenir vendors are on site to serve the needs of the visitors, such as those shown above.

ROMAN CATHOLICISM

Most Croats are Roman Catholic, as are the people of neighboring Croatia. Church missionaries began converting Slavic groups in the fifth century CE. The Catholic Church is headed by the pope in Rome, assisted by bishops and archbishops around the world. The pope is regarded as the successor of Saint Peter, the leader of the Apostles, and is seen as the highest authority in the religion. The Bosnian archdiocese is in Sarajevo, and there are bishops in Mostar and Banja Luka.

Most Croats, and the few Catholic Serbs, attend Mass on Sunday, and some go to daily Mass. They receive Holy Communion—the wafer and wine that is said to be transformed during Mass into the body and blood of Jesus Christ. Other sacraments include baptism, confession, marriage, and anointing of the sick. Catholics believe in the Holy Trinity, which is the concept of one God in three persons—the Father, Son, and Holy Ghost (or Holy Spirit).

INTERNET LINKS

https://www.aljazeera.com/indepth/features/increase-anti -bosnian-anti-muslim-bigotry-report-190923053105055.html
A 2018 report found a rise in anti-Bosniak rhetoric in BiH.

https://www.theatlantic.com/international/archive/2019/01/ bosnia-offers-model-liberal-european-islam/579529
A Bosniak writer argues that a modern, liberal interpretation of Islam is compatible with European culture.

https://theculturetrip.com/europe/bosnia-herzegovina/articles/ the-most-beautiful-religious-buildings-in-bosnia-herzegovina
Some of Bosnia's most extraordinary churches, mosques, and a synagogue are highlighted on this site.

https://www.theguardian.com/world/2016/may/06/banja-luka -mosque-bosnia-herzegovina-serbia-reopens-reconstruction
This is the story of the rebuilding of the Ferhad Pasha Mosque in Banja Luka.

LANGUAGE
Bosna i Hercegovina
Босна и Херцеговина

A road sign marks the border between Bosnia and Croatia in both the Latin and Cyrillic alphabets.

9

BOSNIA HAS THREE OFFICIAL languages—Bosnian, Serbian, and Croatian. The languages are very similar. In fact, they are more or less the same language. Throughout much of the 20th century, that language was called Serbo-Croatian, and Yugoslav officials enforced its use in an effort to unite the people of Yugoslavia. However, the term Serbo-Croatian is no longer used. So now, in the post-Yugoslavia era, Bosnia has three main ethnicities, and therefore three official languages—the Bosniaks speak Bosnian, the Croats speak Croatian, and the Serbs speak Serbian. Are they really just one language with three names? This is a matter of much contention.

Linguistics is the scientific study of language. Linguists usually say that if a speaker of Language A and a speaker of Language B cannot understand each other, then A and B are different languages. By that definition, Bosnian, Serbian, and Croatian—as well as Montenegrin, the official language of Montenegro—are all one language, albeit with various

In 1492, when Spain expelled the Jews, many who fled ended up in Bosnia. They took with them their language, a medieval form of Spanish called Ladino or Judeo-Spanish. In BiH, it's called Djidio. Prior to World War II and the Holocaust, Sarajevo's Jewish community had a Djidio-language newspaper. Today, however, only a handful speak the language, which is on the verge of extinction.

A woman works at a newspaper stand in Trebinje that carries both Latin- and Cyrillic-alphabet publications.

dialects. Indeed, a speaker of one of Bosnia's three languages can understand the other two.

(For perspective, consider a situation in which the people of Britain, Australia, Canada, and the United States declared they spoke four different languages—British, Australian, Canadian, and American.)

The people of Bosnia and Herzegovina have spoken basically the same language for more than a thousand years. However, today most Bosnians, Serbs, and Croats insist that their language is uniquely their own. This is because language is more than just the way people speak and write. It's a cultural expression that is deeply intertwined with literature, ideas, history, and a people's sense of identity. It's hard to separate language from nationalism and politics.

The Cyrillic alphabet, like the Latin alphabet, has capital and lowercase versions of each letter, but the lowercase letters are mostly just small versions of the uppercase ones. Like the Latin alphabet, it is read left to right, and it also has a cursive writing style.

Cyrillic is sometimes incorrectly called the Russian alphabet, because it is used in Russia. It is also used throughout Central Asia and in parts of Eastern Europe.

However, Cyrillic is slightly different in the various countries that use it. For example, the Russian alphabet has 32 letters, while the Serbian alphabet has 30.

А а   Б б   В в
Г г   Д д   Ђ ђ
Е е   Ж ж   З з   И и
Ј ј   К к   Л л   Љ љ
М м   Н н   Њ њ
О о   П п   Р р   С с
Т т   Ћ ћ   У у
Ф ф   Х х   Ц ц
Ч ч   Џ џ   Ш ш

ONE LANGUAGE, TWO ALPHABETS

To make matters even more confusing, the one (or four) language(s) that was once called Serbo-Croatian uses two alphabets: the Latin, or Roman, alphabet that is used in English and other Western languages, and Cyrillic, which is used in Russia, Ukraine, and several other Eastern European, Balkan, and Central Asian nations. Bosniaks and Croats use the Latin alphabet, while Serbs tend to use Cyrillic.

The division between the Croatian and Serbian writing systems originated in the 11th century, when both groups converted to Christianity. The Serbs were aligned with the Eastern Orthodox Church, which used the Cyrillic alphabet. The Croats followed the Roman Catholic Church and its use of the Latin alphabet.

CYRIL AND METHODIUS

A Byzantine icon of Saints Cyril and Methodius glorifies the brothers who brought the written word to the Slavs.

In 863 CE, two Greek brothers—Cyril and Methodius—were sent to the Slavic lands by the patriarch of the Eastern Orthodox Church. The two monks were brilliant scholars and linguists, and their mission was to Christianize the southern Slavs. At the time, the Slavs did not have a written language. Therefore, to acquaint the Slavic-speaking peoples with the Bible, the brothers invented an alphabet, now called Cyrillic, based on the Greek alphabet. Since Slavic languages were rich in sounds, the brothers found they needed 43 letters, a number that has since been reduced. In creating this alphabet, the monks brought literacy to the Slavic people, and they are still revered in the Balkans for that reason.

The brothers were eventually made saints in both the Eastern Orthodox and Roman Catholic branches of Christianity for Christianizing many Slavic peoples and for influencing the cultural development of those peoples. Together, Saint Cyril and Saint Methodius have the title of "the Apostles of the Slavs."

The Cyrillic alphabet is still used in Russian, Ukrainian, and Bulgarian, as well as in the Serbian variant of Serbo-Croatian. Cyrillic remains the official alphabet of the Serbian Republic, and it is also used in North Macedonia. Croats and Bosniaks continue to use the Roman (or Latin) alphabet, the same alphabet that is used throughout Europe and the Americas.

PRONUNCIATION

Bosnian and Croatian, using the Roman alphabet, and Serbian, using the Cyrillic alphabet, are pronounced as they are written, and every letter is pronounced.

Some letters, especially those with accent marks and pairs of letters, have special sounds.

Some special letters

c	*sounds like the* ts *in cats*
č	*sounds like the* ch *sound in cello*
ć	*sounds like the* tch *in latch*
đ	*sounds like* dya
dz	*sounds like the* j *in just*
j	*sounds like the* y *in young*
š	*like the* sh *in mush*
nj	*sounds like* nya
ž	*sounds like the* s *in pleasure*

Some words in Bosnian

selo	*village*
pesma	*song*
reka	*river*
da	*yes*
ne	*no*
adravo	*hello*
dovidenja	*goodbye*

Some phrases in Bosnian

Zovem se	*My name is …*
Kako se zovete?	*What's your name?*
Gavorite li engleski?	*Do you speak English?*
Kada brod polazi?	*What time does the boat leave?*
Kada voz (or vlak in Croatian) dolazi?	*What time does the train arrive?*
Hvala..	*Thank you.*

Bosnian Muslims greet each other with a handshake and a kiss on the cheek.

Although local dialects introduce variations in how words sound, there are a few general rules. The position of the stress in a word is never on the last syllable, and in most words the accent falls on the first vowel.

NONVERBAL COMMUNICATION

Each of Bosnia's three ethnic-religious groups has certain ways of communicating without words that may be different from those of the other groups.

In the Serb Republic, for example, people greet one another with three kisses—first on the left cheek, then the right, and a third on the left. In Sarajevo, and in other parts of the Bosniak-Croat Federation, the greeting is a single kiss on each cheek.

Customs are also a way to communicate respect. If you visit a Muslim's home, for instance, it would be insulting to keep your shoes on. Instead, the guest is expected to remove his or her shoes and wait for the host to provide a pair of slippers. Similarly, people leave their footwear outside before entering a mosque to maintain the mosque's cleanliness and sanctity.

INTERNET LINKS

http://www.bbc.com/travel/story/20181017-the-bosnians-who -speak-medieval-spanish
This is the story of the Landino language.

https://www.economist.com/the-economist-explains/2017/04/10/ is-serbo-croatian-a-language
This article considers whether Serbo-Croatian is a language.

https://www.equaltimes.org/the-politics-of-language-in -bosnia?lang=en#.Xh9oHchKjcs
This article explains the politics of language in Bosnia.

https://www.omniglot.com/writing/bosnian.htm
https://www.omniglot.com/writing/croatian.htm
https://www.omniglot.com/writing/serbian.htm
This language site provides an introduction to the Bosnian, Croatian, and Serbian languages.

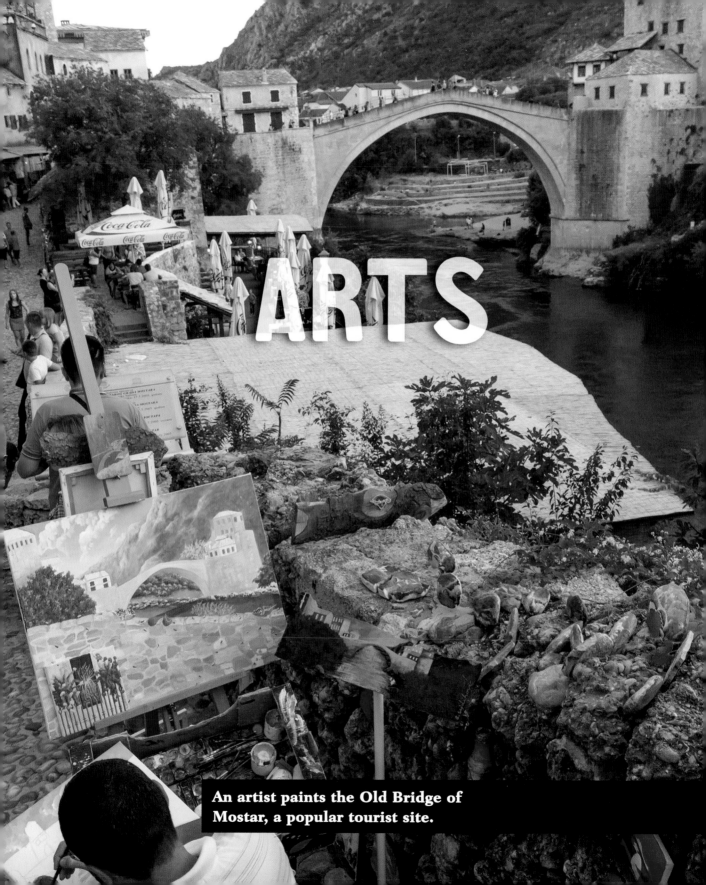

ARTS

An artist paints the Old Bridge of Mostar, a popular tourist site.

10

LITERATURE, THE ARTS, AND handicrafts all have a long and distinguished history in Bosnia and Herzegovina. The nation is at the crossroads between Europe and the Islamic world of the Middle East, so several cultures have shaped and influenced its artistic development. Music in Bosnia today, for example, ranges from ancient Turkish melodies to Balkan, or Slavic, folk songs to modern jazz and various kinds of rock, electronica, pop, and hip-hop music—and some kinds that mix several genres.

The country and its artists are recognized far beyond the Balkan Peninsula. For instance, the Sarajevo Film Festival, held each August, draws filmmakers and actors from all over the world, and the city's Poetry Days has become one of the great international gatherings of poets. In addition, a number of Bosnian crafts, such as metalworking and weaving, are world renowned.

LITERATURE AND POETRY

In the 19th century, Bosnian writers played an important part in the growing movements for independence, using their literary powers to

The National Gallery of Bosnia and Herzegovina in Sarajevo houses a collection of art from the former Yugoslavia, as well as more contemporary pieces. Another important museum of contemporary art in the city is Ars Aevi, which was established as part of a cultural resistance movement during the Siege of Sarajevo.

The Festina Lente Bridge over the Miljacka River in Sarajevo opened in 2012. Behind it stands the Academy of Fine Arts.

protest rule by outsiders—the Ottoman Turks. A monk named Ivan Franjo Jukic started the country's first literary journal, *Bosanski Prijatelj* (*Bosnian Friend*), which spread the voice of protest throughout the Slavic countries.

The 20th century was a time of great literary creativity throughout the country. Bosniak, Serb, and Croat writers dealt with their own group's nationalistic aspirations and the need to drive out foreign influences—both Turkey and Austria-Hungary. Mesa Selimovic and Ivo Andric were Bosnians, and both wrote novels describing the evils of repressive governments. In spite of their Bosnian roots, both were associated with the drive to create a greater Yugoslavia blending various groups.

VISUAL ARTS

At the end of the 19th century, with Austro-Hungarian rule in Bosnia cemented, the visual arts began to show the influence of contemporary Europe. Young artists traveled throughout Europe, studying the styles of expressionism and impressionism. The 1950s and later decades brought to light a number of conceptual artists, including Braco Dimitrijevic. Cultural life in Bosnia's cities flourished through the 1960s and 1970s. Many institutions, including the Academy of Fine Arts in Sarajevo, were established at this time.

During the Siege of Sarajevo, some artists, such as the painter Safet Zec, fled the country. Those who didn't or who couldn't made a concerted effort to continue working, but it was a risky business. Architect and artist Vesna Bugarski refused to leave Sarajevo during the siege and died in August 1992 at age 62, killed by a grenade. Looters then ransacked her house and stole her work.

Yet it was possible to attend art exhibitions, as well as theatrical and musical events, throughout the war. In spite of Bosnia's wartime isolation from the

Ivo Andric (1892–1975) was the son of Catholic Croats, born in the central region of today's Federation of Bosnia and Herzegovina. At the time, Bosnia was part of the Austro-Hungarian Empire. When World War I broke out, Andric was jailed for his anti-Austrian activities. After the war, in 1923, he entered the Yugoslav diplomatic service, and for a while he served in Berlin, Germany. When Germany invaded Yugoslavia in 1941, he returned home.

He began his literary career as a poet, but he soon turned to prose. He hit his stride during World War II with two outstanding novels: Travnicka Hronika *(1945; published in English in 1959 as* Bosnian Story*), and the book now considered his masterpiece,* Na Drini Cuprija *(*The Bridge on the Drina*, 1945). This novel focuses on the town of Visegrad in eastern Bosnia (in today's Republika Srpska) and its famous Mehmed Pasa Sokolovic Bridge over the Drina River. The bridge, now a UNESCO World Heritage site, is the story's main character. The novel follows the bridge from its construction during the Ottoman occupation in the 1570s through the outbreak of the First World War. Along the way, Andric vividly describes the history of Bosnia as seen from this unusual perspective.*

His best writing drew on the ethnic diversity of his native country. His novels, including The Woman of Sarajevo *(1945), explored Bosnia's history and the ongoing clash between East and West. In 1961, he was awarded the Nobel Prize for Literature, the highest award an author can achieve. His work was praised by the Nobel Prize committee for its "epic force" and for the "great beauty and purity" of his language.*

In spite of his great fame, Andric has been severely criticized—mostly by Bosniaks, who feel his writing is anti-Muslim. Federation authorities have removed his novels from many libraries and schools. In 1992, a Bosniak nationalist in Visegrad destroyed a statue of Andric with a sledgehammer. (It was replaced in 2012, shown above.)

international art scene, several art institutions were formed at this time, such as the Sarajevo Center for Contemporary Arts, a nonprofit organization that deals with the promotion and development of the country's contemporary visual arts.

Wartime destruction led to a lack of gallery space in Sarajevo. As a result, some artists used the city itself as their exhibition space. So-called public, site-specific art can be found throughout Sarajevo.

FILM

One of Europe's great film directors, Bosnian Emir Kusturica, has had experiences similar to Ivo Andric's. Kusturica, a Muslim, set his films in Sarajevo. He won the Golden Lion Award at the 1981 Venice Film Festival for the film *Do You Remember Dolly Bell?* His reputation soared in 1985 when his film *When Father Was Away on Business* was nominated for an Academy Award as the year's best foreign film. However, *Underground* (1995), considered his greatest film, was condemned in Sarajevo for being anti-Muslim. Angry and frustrated, Kusturica left the city. In 2005, he joined the Serbian Orthodox Church and has lived in Serbia since then. His most recent film, as of early 2020, is *El Pepe: A Supreme Life* (2018).

Another outstanding Bosnian filmmaker is Danis Tanovic. Born in Zenica, Tanovic made a striking film about the civil war, actually shooting the scenes in Slovenia and Italy because it was safer. The film, *No Man's Land*, is the story of two soldiers—a Serb and a Muslim—during the Siege of Sarajevo. It won the Palme d'Or Award at the 2001 Cannes Film Festival and an Academy Award as Best Foreign Film in 2002. His most recent film as of early 2020 is *Death in Sarajevo* (2016).

MUSIC

Music in Bosnia and Herzegovina is a delightful mixture of the old and the new, the West and the East. The country's music includes a variety of musical styles that combine old-time folk songs with newer sounds. A traditional type of song, called *ravne pesme* (RAHV-nay PEE-es-mee), is very flat, almost tuneless; in

its more modern guise, called *ganga* (GHAN-gah), it sounds to the uninitiated like someone shouting a rap song.

During the 45 years of Communist Party rule, the government did not approve of Western music—that is, the music of Western Europe and the United States. In fact, much of the time this "decadent" music was not allowed—on the radio or in live performances. The government did encourage folk music, and those traditional songs and melodies have been passed down from one generation to the other and remain very popular today.

Bosnian instruments also represent a mixture, primarily a blending of West and East. The traditional folk songs of rural villages are often played on unusual instruments, such as a Bosnian wooden flute or a bagpipe called a *diple*.

Traditional urban music, like the rural folk songs, has an Asian or Middle Eastern sound. These songs are sometimes difficult to perform—especially to sing—because there can be more than one musical note for each syllable,

A group of Bosnian musicians perform traditional fare in front of the historic Sebilj Fountain in Sarajevo.

Probably Bosnia's most famous contemporary musician, Dino Merlin is a singer-songwriter and record producer whose music spans genres from pop to rock and beyond. He plays a number of instruments and performs internationally. He is one of Bosnia's most commercially successful artists. Born Edin Dervishalidovic, he is known by his stage name, Dino Merlin, which explains his nickname, "The Wizard."

As a young man growing up in a Muslim family, he began his singing career as the muezzin at his local mosque. A muezzin sings to call the faithful to prayer. He started his first band in high school and went on to form the band Merlin, which released its first album in 1985. In 1991, Dervishalidovic took

Dino Merlin performs in the semifinals of the Eurovision Song Contest 2011 in Dusseldorf, Germany.

the stage name Dino Merlin and has recorded six studio albums under that name. Some members of the band Merlin were killed during the civil war, which led him to write the song "Sva Bol Sviljeta" ("All the Grief in the World").

Although Dino Merlin performs globally, in the Balkan region, he is a superstar. He regularly sells out stadium concerts. His most recent album is Hotel Nacional, *released in 2014.*

but performers are able to work miracles with a remarkable one-string fiddle called a *gusla*. For centuries, the gusla has been used to accompany a storyteller narrating and singing an epic poem. The most popular folk songs, both rural and urban, are called *sevdalinka*. These are highly emotional love songs, usually telling of the great tragedy of a love lost or, occasionally, of finding one's great love.

Since 1990, the music of the West has become increasingly popular. Young people flock to nightclubs and jazz clubs to dance or just to listen to the latest European and US hits.

Today, one of the most popular places in Bosnia is the Pavarotti Music Center in Mostar. The music center was created in 1997 mostly through charitable contributions to provide a place for the children of Bosnia to learn about, perform, and enjoy music. It was conceived as a haven to escape the physical and emotional aftermath of war. Today, it offers courses in music, filmmaking, photography, and acting.

DANCE

In communist Yugoslavia, traditional folk dancing was sponsored by the state, and there were more than 300 amateur folk dancing groups. Today, Bosnian traditional folk dances are perhaps the least known of all the regional folk dances of the former parts of Yugoslavia.

A popular folk dance called *nijemo kolo* (nee-YAY-moh KOH-loh) is performed without music. Instead, the rhythmic stamping of feet and the jingling of coins sewn into women's aprons or skirts accompany this dance, which is performed with great speed and dexterity. In many folk dances, men and women form separate lines, similar to square dancing or line dancing in parts of the United States.

As with music, interest in these traditional dance forms is diminishing due to the influence of the modern era and Western popular culture.

People browse displays of arts and crafts on the cobbled streets of the Old Town section of Mostar.

CRAFTS

Bosnia and Herzegovina has a long, proud handicraft tradition, particularly in textiles, metalworking, and woodworking, all dating back to the rule of the Ottoman Turks in the 15th and 16th centuries. When working with textiles, some craftspeople worked in their cottages, while others had separate stalls or shops in a domed building called a *bezistan* (BEZZ-ih-stahn).

WEAVING   Bosnian weavers employed techniques and designs from Persia (modern Iran) to create exquisite rugs and wall hangings. Using a design drawn on paper, the workers took painstaking care to weave the complex design into wool cloth. Until the late 1800s, only natural dyes were used—from plants, such as indigo; from minerals, such as ocher; and from animal life, including certain

Just as UNESCO works to protect natural and cultural World Heritage sites, it also identifies examples of the "intangible cultural heritage of humanity" that need to be preserved. These include, according to the group's website, "traditions or living expressions inherited from our ancestors and passed on to our descendants, such as oral traditions, performing arts, social practices, rituals, arts, festive events, knowledge and practices concerning nature and the universe or the knowledge and skills to produce traditional crafts."

The Convention for the Safeguarding of the Intangible Cultural Heritage has listed three entries for Bosnia and Herzegovnia: Zmijanje embroidery, Konjic woodcarving, and the picking of iva grass on Mount Ozren.

insects. These natural dyes produced many subtle shadings that artificial dyes could not duplicate, and the resulting colors were rich and long-lasting.

Another unique feature of the weaving is the hand knotting of the yarn around the warp yarns. Creating the luxurious pile of a true Persian rug could require more than 2,000 knots per square inch! On rare occasions, Bosnian weavers worked with exotic fabrics such as velvet or silk, often with threads of silver and gold.

EMBROIDERY   Bosnian craftspeople are also famous for their embroidery, stitching colorful designs on women's blouses and aprons, men's traditional clothes, scarves and shawls, pillowcases, and other items.

The most common designs are geometric patterns, sometimes incorporating plant life, such as blossoms, leaves, and stems. Bosnian women learn to embroider at a very young age, and the needlework is very much part of the culture. One specific kind of embroidery, practiced in the Manjaca Mountain region of Republika Srpska, is recognized by UNESCO on its Intangible Cultural Heritage of Humanity List. This Zmijanje embroidery technique uses blue threads on white in characteristic geometric designs. It is crafted only by women, often in groups, and is featured in the traditional folk costumes of the region.

A craftsman hammers designs into a copper dish in his small shop in the Mostar bazaar.

METALWORKING

In Eastern-style bazaars in Mostar, Sarajevo, and other cities, skilled metalworkers sit in their small, cluttered shops hammering elaborate designs in brass or copper to be used for household items such as coffeepots, trays, bowls, and jewelry. Some towns are known for the specialization of their metalworkers. They sometimes work on larger metal items, such as doors and gates. Some metalworkers specialize in filigree—using thin, twisted wires of copper, silver, or gold. Others focus on techniques such as embossing—creating a raised design.

WOODWORKING

This is another highly refined craft. Ornate carvings are used in the interiors of houses, including moldings, doors, furniture, and paneling. Mosques and minarets also feature elaborate wood carvings. As in other forms of Islamic art, there are no representations of humans, but floral shapes are common, as are designs based on calligraphy.

In 2017, Konjic woodcarving was added to UNESCO's Intangible Cultural Heritage of Humanity List. The craft has a long tradition in the mostly Bosniak town of Konjic in the Federation of BiH. The region, in northern Herzegovina, is mountainous and heavily wooded. At both the professional and hobby level, the intricate hand-carving of furniture and decorative objects is a valued part of the local culture and is practiced by men and women.

POTTERY In the Bosnian countryside, traditional potters produce pieces using an ancient method that is extinct elsewhere. The mineral calcite is added to the clay, which is formed into pots on a hand-operated wheel. The pots are often fired on a bonfire. This technique died out throughout the rest of Europe several centuries ago. The pots are in great demand for use in traditional Bosnian cooking. Potters using this method can still be found working in several towns in Bosnia and Herzegovina. In Ljesevo, near Sarajevo, a different style is represented where fancier pots are kiln-fired and decorated.

INTERNET LINKS

https://balkaninsight.com/2017/09/29/sarajevo-s-metalworkers-revive-their-craft-09-29-2017
This article examines the revival of metalworking as a craft in Bosnia.

http://www.dinomerlin.com/biografija?b=eng
Bosnian music star Dino Merlin's official website is partly available in English.

https://ich.unesco.org/en/RL/konjic-woodcarving-01288
https://ich.unesco.org/en/RL/zmijanje-embroidery-00990
Photos of Konjic woodcarvings and Zmijanje embroidery are presented on these UNESCO Intangible Cultural Heritage listings.

https://theculturetrip.com/europe/bosnia-herzegovina/articles/bosnian-pop-music-in-8-artists
This 2017 article lists some of Bosnia's top pop artists.

LEISURE

A little boy prepares to ride his bike on a sidewalk in Bileca.

11

BOSNIANS SPEND A LOT OF TIME with their families, enjoying large meals on Sundays and holidays, usually followed by a walk through the downtown of their small cities. (Even Sarajevo, by far the largest city, has fewer than 350,000 people.)

People enjoy shopping, and shopping malls are a recent addition, especially in the rebuilt cities and suburbs. As in the United States and Western Europe, young people like to simply hang out, but anything that looks like loitering is not approved of. Bands and theatrical groups often provide entertainment. In cafés or at home, people play chess and card games. Like most folks everywhere, Bosnians enjoy relaxing at home—watching TV, surfing the internet, catching up on the news, or following a favorite sports team.

For more vigorous entertainment, Bosnia's many forests, streams, and mountains provide ample opportunity for hunting, hiking, rafting, and skiing, among other outdoor activities.

HUNTING

Bosnia, like other mountainous regions of southeastern Europe, has been considered a sportsman's paradise for centuries. Wealthy Europeans and members of the nobility have come to this part of the Balkans to hunt several prized animals, such as the ever-dangerous wild boar, the European bison, and the Carpathian red deer—a large deer known for its huge antlers.

A hunter takes aim in a forest in Doboj.

However, the popularity of hunting in these primitive-looking forests has contributed to the disappearance, or near disappearance, of some species. For instance, the aurochs, a large wild ox, is extinct, and the European bison, slightly larger but lighter than the North American species, was reduced to fewer than a dozen animals in private collections by the 1930s. They have been used to start a new breeding herd, with some interbreeding with North American bison, but none have been reintroduced into the wild in Bosnia.

In a strange way, the popularity of some game animals may contribute to their survival. The Herzegovinian brown bear, for example, is a big, lumbering creature that has retreated deep into the Dinaric Alps. Income from hunting permits provides revenue that is helping to establish reserves to protect the remaining bears. In addition, conservation efforts have helped some hunted species make a comeback, including the lynx.

The hunting of game birds has also led to the decline of several species. The black grouse, for example, was hunted almost to extinction before conservation programs began to reverse the trend in the 1970s.

WATER SPORTS AND FISHING

The rushing streams of Bosnia and Herzegovina draw white-water rafters from many countries. The Una River near Bihac is famous for its long stretches of rapids. There was heavy fighting in and around Bihac during the civil war, but nearly all the damage has been repaired and the area seems to be clear of land mines. The rafting season runs from May through October, and the Una Regatta is held for two weeks in July.

The spectacular Bosnian scenery, with its challenging mountains and sparkling rivers, also draws outdoor enthusiasts for fishing. Some remote fishing lodges have pampered guests for 100 years or more. In addition to

In 1984, Sarajevo hosted the Winter Olympics. The city was then a part of Yugoslavia, which that year became the first communist nation to host a Winter Games. (Moscow was the first communist Olympic city. It had hosted the Summer Olympics in 1980, which was boycotted by the United States and 65 other nations to protest the Soviet war in Afghanistan.) The selection of Sarajevo as the 1984 Olympic site was in recognition of the sports-mindedness of the people and the availability of natural sites for events like downhill and cross-country skiing.

Athletes ride a luge in the Sarajevo Olympics. Below, the track's current condition is shown.

The games were a success—1,272 athletes from 49 countries competed in 39 events. East Germany (Germany was divided in those days) and the Soviet Union dominated the medal count, but individual records were achieved as well. Among the many highlights, Slovenian skier Jure Franko won Yugoslavia's first Winter Olympic medal, earning a silver in the giant slalom, and British ice dancers Jayne Torvill and Christopher Dean earned perfect scores for artistic impression for their ice dancing performance to Maurice Ravel's Bolero. The dazzling event gave no indication that just a few years later, Sarajevo would become a great casualty in a brutal civil war.

Today, many of Sarajevo's formerly grand Olympic venues stand abandoned, crumbling, or destroyed by the war. The bobsled and luge track in the hills above the city

was used as a Bosnian-Serb artillery stronghold during the Siege of Sarajevo. The ski jumping venue on Mount Igman was used as an artillery range. The luge track was covered in graffiti, and the ski jumps were riddled with bullet holes. Other venues are ghostly ruins. Nevertheless, even though the games were a long time ago now, Sarajevo residents still take pride in remembering them.

Sportsmen compete in a fishing contest on Modrac Lake in the Lukavac region.

rushing trout streams, Bosnia's two large lakes, Jablanica Jezero and Busko Jezero, are considered outstanding for bass and other game fish.

UNUSUAL GAME FISH   Bosnia also has some unusual fish that lure sports fishers who want to try something new. The huchen, for example, is a large troutlike fish that reaches lengths of 5 feet (1.5 m) and a weight of 110 pounds (50 kilograms). Other unusual game fish are the gudgeon and the catfish-like loach.

SPORTS

Bosnians enjoy a variety of individual and team sports. Skiing has long been popular in the region, and people can still enjoy some of the downhill slopes groomed for the Olympics. Sledding and ice-skating are also popular, and hockey is gaining a larger following every year.

Like most Europeans, Bosnians are crazy for soccer (known to them as football). During the war in the 1990s, the Bosnian soccer league broke into three comparatively weak divisions along ethnic lines, with Bosniak, Serb, and Croat teams mostly playing against teams from their own ethnic-religious group. Today, however, there is one league and one men's national team. In 2014, the national team qualified to play in the FIFA World Cup, but that was the only time since independence that it has done so. In addition, there is club soccer, with clubs across the country playing professionally against each other.

Basketball is also very popular. The Basketball Federation of Bosnia and Herzegovina oversees close to 150 basketball clubs in the country, with more than 5,000 registered players. There are both professional and amateur teams,

The Bosnian national team is shown here during a 2014 World Cup game. The World Cup is soccer's most famous tournament.

National soccer team goalkeeper Asmir Begovic plays with a child at a newly built playground in Sarajevo. The athlete's charity organization, the Asmir Begovic Foundation, funded the construction of the playground.

and people closely follow the careers of players who have made it to the US National Basketball Association (NBA). Some of them include Ivica Zubac, Dzanan Musa, and Dragan Bender.

TAKING GAMES TO THE STREETS   Kids throughout the country play pickup soccer games in parks, parking lots, fields, and in the streets. Many schools and clubs have teams. The televising of professional games and World Cup matches has contributed to the popularity of the sport.

Basketball is a late arrival in Bosnia and Herzegovina, but it is growing with remarkable speed among young Bosnians. Backboards and rims (with or without nets) are seen everywhere in parks and on neighborhood utility poles. Other outdoor sports include skateboarding and in-line skating. Cycling is also popular, including road races similar to the Tour de France, which is an annual world cycling race.

ENTERTAINMENT

The people of Bosnia and Herzegovina have been fond of American music for several generations. Even during the austere communist days, goodwill tours by Louis Armstrong and other great jazz figures were well received. By the 1980s, all forms of American music were played in dance clubs and jazz clubs. Young people flocked to these places, usually for live music, although today, DJs are becoming more common. Homegrown music stars now have tremendous followings.

INTERNET LINKS

https://basketball.realgm.com/nba/birth-countries/22/Bosnia -and-Herzegovina
This page lists the Bosnian basketball players in the NBA.

https://www.olympic.org/sarajevo-1984
https://www.olympic.org/news/sarajevo-84-the-human-legacy -that-has-stood-the-test-of-time
These pages on the Olympic Games website offer highlights of the Sarajevo Games (top URL), and the venue's destruction and rebuilding (bottom URL).

https://theconversation.com/when-bosnia-was-torn-apart-football -clubs-were-ethnically-cleansed-along-with-the-population-80913
This article discusses how the war in Bosnia affected its soccer clubs.

FESTIVALS

A colorful parade draws a crowd in Bijeljina, in the Republika Srpska.

12

THE PRESENCE OF THREE RELIGIONS in the country provides Bosnia with a colorful array of festivals, holidays, and holy days. There are also several holidays that have been imported in recent years through travel or even internet contact. Earth Day, with posters and picnics promoting environmental protection, is celebrated in several towns in early April. Halloween is another recent import, with many kids copying costume ideas they see on television.

Two religions will sometimes honor the same holiday, but in quite different ways. Both the Roman Catholic Church and the Eastern Orthodox Church celebrate Christmas and Easter, but their observances are quite different. Both also honor Saints Cyril and Methodius, but the Catholics honor them in April, and the Eastern Orthodox in May.

Secular festivals are also varied. Independence Day for the Federation of Bosnia and Herzegovina is March 1, for example, the date Bosnia separated from Yugoslavia. Bosnian Serbs in the Republika Srpska do not honor this date, preferring their own national holidays instead.

Participants in an international folklore festival parade down a street in Lukavac.

Spring is a time to celebrate the renewal of life and the anticipation of a new crop year. For Serbs and Croats, the celebration is Djurdjevdan, a time to celebrate the fertility and renewal of the land. The festival—complete with food, music, and dances—is most important in farming villages.

PATRIOTIC HOLIDAYS

There is no shared patriotic holiday in Bosnia and Herzegovnia that is observed in all of its entities. The Republika Srpska observes Victory Day on May 9, in honor of triumph over Nazi Germany in 1945, and Dayton Agreement Day on November 21. It also celebrates January 9, Day of Republika Srpska, which

January 1, 2 . . . . .New Year's Day . . . . .All
January 6. . . . . .Orthodox Christmas Eve . . . . .RS
January 7. . . . . .Orthodox Christmas Day. . . . . .RS
January 9. . . . . .Day of the Republika Srpska . . . . . . .RS
January 14 . . . . .Orthodox New Year . . . . .RS
March 1 . . . . .Independence Day . . . . .FBiH
March 8 . . . . .Brcko District Establishment Day . . . . Brcko District
March–April (changeable) . . . . .Catholic Good Friday,
. . . . .Easter Sunday, Monday. . . . . .FBiH
later March–April (changeable) . .Orthodox Good Friday,
. . . . .Easter Sunday, Monday. . . . . .RS
May 1. . . . . .Labor Day . . . . .All
May 9. . . . . .Victory Day . . . . .RS
November 1 . . . . .All Saints' Day. . . . . .FBiH
November 21. . . . . .Dayton Peace Agreement Day . . . . . .RS
November 25. . . . . .Statehood Day. . . . . .FBiH
December 25 . . . . .Catholic Christmas Day . . . . .FBiH
Islamic holidays (changeable). . . .End of Ramadan (Eid al-Fitr),
. . . . .Feast of the Sacrifice (Eid al-Adha) . . .FBiH

was deemed unconstitutional by the BiH Constitutional Court in 2015. The event marks the anniversary of the creation of Republika Srpska in 1992, an occasion that many Bosniaks see as the precursor to the outbreak of the war a few months later. Despite the holiday having been banned following the court ruling, the people of the RS voted overwhelmingly in 2016 in favor of keeping it. Since then, the illegal observance has been celebrated in Banja Luka and other cities with parades, award ceremonies, speeches by politicians, and much flag waving.

The Federation of Bosnia and Herzegovina entity, meanwhile, marks March 1 as its Independence Day and Statehood Day on November 25.

MUSLIM RELIGIOUS HOLIDAYS

The most important event in Islam is the month-long fast of Ramadan—observed during the ninth month of the lunar calendar. It is the month when the Prophet Muhammad received the words of the Quran. Every day of this month is a time of prayer and reflection, and Muslims are expected to fast, or refrain from eating and drinking, during daylight hours. Because Muslims follow a lunar calendar rather than the Western solar calendar, the dates of Ramadan change from year to year.

Ramadan is also a time to celebrate with family and friends. As soon as the sun goes down, Bosniaks break the fast with a prayer and a meal—the *iftar* (EEF-tar). The streets are filled with people visiting family and friends or enjoying Turkish coffee and baklava at an outdoor café.

When the month of fasting ends, there is a three-day holiday and celebration called Eid al-Fitr, the Feast of the Fast Breaking. This celebration is also known as Bajram. People gather with family and close friends for three days of feasting. Many Bosniaks exchange gifts, and a number of towns have street fairs, with food stalls and live music. The minarets are decorated with strings of electric lights.

CHRISTIAN RELIGIOUS HOLIDAYS

Christmas and Easter are the principal religious holidays for all branches of Christianity, although the forms of celebration differ. Bosnia's Roman Catholics, mostly Croats, celebrate Christmas much as other Europeans and Americans do, although with a good deal less commercialism. While families may have a Christmas tree, for example, decorations and gifts are more modest.

On June 29, 2019, horseback riders led a procession celebrating the 509th anniversary of the Muslim festival "Days of Ajvatovica." The event in Prusac, Bosnia, commemorates a miracle in 1510 in which a religious man named Ajvaz-Dedo prayed to Allah for a source of clean water for the village and had his prayers answered. Today's faithful visit the holy site every June.

The Eastern Orthodox Christmas is slightly different, including the date, which is in early January rather than on December 25. There are also regional variations in the celebration. For instance, while many families cut a traditional pine or spruce for their Christmas tree, families in some regions choose a young oak for a Yule tree, or *badnjak* (BAHD-nyak). The oak symbolizes both the cross on which Jesus was crucified and also the new life that will come in the spring. (The oak holds its leaves far longer than other trees, often until late in the winter.) The lower part of the trunk is cut and burned as a Yule log, while the branches are decorated with ribbons, fruit, and candy. Straw is spread around the base of the tree for the manger in which the baby Jesus was born, and more straw is spread around the festive table.

The Eastern Orthodox Easter is held from one to five weeks after the Roman Catholic and Protestant Easter. The standard Easter greeting is "Christ is Risen." Orthodox families place an Easter cake in a basket, with painted eggs, butter, and cheese, and take it to the church for the priest's blessing.

Bosnian Serbs also celebrate Krsna Slava—a sort of collective birthday, also called Saint George's Day in some parts of the country. Every family has a patron saint, usually a figure from far back in history. For more than half the families, Saint George is the family patron, and the saint's day is to commemorate the time when the family, or its tribal group, was baptized into the Orthodox faith. Bosnian Serbs celebrate the day with street fairs and music. As on Easter, they take holiday cakes to the local church for a priestly blessing.

INTERNET LINKS

https://balkaninsight.com/2020/01/09/bosnian-serbs-mark-illegal-holiday-with-grand-parade
This article, with several photos, describes the 2020 celebration of Day of Republika Srpska.

https://www.timeanddate.com/holidays/bosnia
This calendar site lists the public holidays, local holidays, and observances in the three entities of BiH.

FOOD

A woman purchases fruit at a produce market in Sarajevo.

13

B OSNIAN FOODS REFLECT THE history and culture of the Balkan region. Both Eastern and Western cuisines show up in the culinary mix, with Mediterranean, Eastern European, and Middle Eastern notes predominating. As in other Balkan countries, the food tends to be heavy and rich, with an emphasis on meat and potatoes or bread.

Supermarket chains have sprung up across much of the country, but street vendors and open-air markets are still popular in many cities. These are often the best places to find the freshest produce, dairy products, and meats, and they often offer lower prices as well.

TRADITIONAL FAVORITES

The Bosnian version of fast food is *cevapcici* (chay-VAHP-chee-chee), which has been popular for nearly 500 years. Called *cevapi* (chay-VA-pee) for short, it is a sausage made of ground lamb, or sometimes beef or pork, and lots of spices, and then grilled with onions. It is often grilled outdoors and served warm on *somun* (SO-moon), a thick pita bread.

If cevapcici is the Bosnian version of a hot dog, then *pljeskavica* (plee-YES-kah-veet-sah) is something like a Balkan hamburger. Prepared much like cevapi, it is formed into patties, much like an American burger.

In the winter, the fragrance of roasted chestnuts fills the air in Sarajevo's Old Town, the Bascarsija. Street vendors roast the nuts in a large pan over a fire and sell the warm snacks in a paper cone.

Grilled mountain trout is one of the few traditional Bosnian fish dishes.

Stuffed vegetables (*dolma*), such as onions, peppers, cabbage leaves (*sarma*), or eggplants, are popular across the Balkans. They are typically stuffed with ground meat or a meat and rice mixture.

Bosnia and Herzegovina has almost no coastline, and seafood and fish are not commonly part of the diet. However, grilled trout (*pastrmka na zaru*) is the exception. Bosnia's many rivers offer fly-fishers an abundance of river trout, and restaurants near such rivers are more likely to offer this specialty.

MEALTIMES

BREAKFAST *Dorucak* (DOE-ru-chak) is a hearty meal to begin the day, and it is served early, with coffee, tea, or warm milk. The typical breakfast

consists of scrambled eggs, a soft white cheese, and bread with butter and jam or honey.

MAIN MEAL *Rucak* (lunch) was once the most substantial meal of the day. Traditionally, most people ate with their family in the afternoon, usually around 2 p.m., followed by a lighter supper in the evening. More and more, though, modern working life prevents that old custom.

When the family can gather for the afternoon meal, it's likely to begin with a hearty homemade soup. This is followed by fish or meat, served with vegetables and salad, and then dessert. Probably the favorite main dish is *bosanski lonac* (BOSS-ahn-skee LON-atz)—a stew made with layers of meat (lamb or beef) and vegetables, slow-roasted and served in a ceramic pot. Other

Burek is beloved all over the Balkans. Here it is served warm, straight from the pan it was made in.

popular dishes include *burek* (BU-rek), a meat- or cheese-filled pastry rolled into a spiral; *japrak* (YA-prak), grape leaves or collard greens stuffed with ground lamb and rice; *sirnica* (SEER-nee-tsa), a flaky pastry filled with soft cheese; and *zeljanica* (zel-YA-nee-tsa), a spinach pie. These stuffed pastries and shish kebab, another favorite, represent the influence of Turkish cuisine.

DESSERTS   Bosnian desserts are usually light, consisting of plain cake or pudding and fresh fruit. Plums are close to being the national fruit and are also used to make *rakija* (RA-kee-ya), a sweet brandy that can also be made with grapes. The former Yugoslavia was one of the world's largest producers of plums.

Baklava with walnuts is a flaky sweet treat.

The most famous dessert in Bosnia and Herzegovina is baklava, which Bosnians eat only on special occasions. This pastry is layered with ground nuts and drenched in a honey syrup. *Tufahije* (tul-FA-hee-ya) is another very sweet dessert made from apples stuffed with chopped walnuts and topped with whipped cream. A confection called *tahan halva* is made from sesame paste, sugar, and ground nuts. It's usually bought at a pastry shop rather than made at home. Another favorite sweet is Turkish delight, or *rahat lokum*, a sticky gel candy cut in squares and rolled in sugar.

BEVERAGES   Kids and young children drink milk or kefir, a thin yogurt drink, and occasionally soft drinks. All beverages are consumed after the main course. Adults have beer or wine, with many local varieties to choose from. After a meal, drinks may be plum brandy, coffee, Bosnian coffee (a stronger drink, similar to Turkish coffee), espresso, or a warm milk-based drink called *salep* (SA-lep).

Normally, Muslims do not drink alcoholic beverages, although this ban was not strictly observed in Bosnia before the civil war. Since the war, however, many Bosniaks have become more strict in their observance of Islamic laws, and some towns have passed laws against serving alcoholic drinks in restaurants and cafés.

INTERNET LINKS

https://theculturetrip.com/europe/bosnia-herzegovina/articles/10-traditional-bosnian-dishes-you-need-to-try
Photos and descriptions of 10 popular Bosnian dishes are presented on this site.

https://www.visitmycountry.net/bosnia_herzegovina/en/index.php/eating-drinking
An overview of Bosnian cuisine is accompanied by links to more detail about special dishes.

CEVAPI (GRILLED SAUSAGES)

These sausages are popular throughout
the Balkans.

¾ pound (350 grams) ground beef
¾ pound (350 g) ground lamb or pork
3 tablespoons finely grated onion
1 tablespoon freshly minced garlic (about
  3 medium cloves)
1 ½ teaspoons paprika
1 ½ teaspoons kosher salt
1 ½ teaspoons freshly ground black pepper
¾ teaspoon baking soda

In a medium bowl, mix together beef, lamb or pork,
onion, garlic, paprika, salt, pepper, and baking soda
by hand until thoroughly combined.

Form meat mixture into finger-length sausages (about 3 inches long by ¾ inch wide, or
7.5 centimeters by 2 centimeters).

With an adult's help, heat grill to medium-high heat. Oil the grilling grate. Grill sausages
over medium-high direct heat until well browned on all sides and just cooked through, about
8 minutes total. Remove to a serving tray or plates, and let rest for 5 minutes.

Serve with grilled pita bread or other flatbread. In Bosnia, it is typically served with chopped
onion and *kajmak*, a thick cream. To approximate this cream, mix ½ cup (75 g) crumbled feta
cheese, 1 cup (240 mL) sour cream, and ½ pound (230 g) softened cream cheese until smooth.

Makes about 6 servings, or 15 cevapi.

TUFAHIJE (POACHED APPLES WITH WALNUTS)

6 apples (choose apples that will hold their
  shape when cooked, such as granny smith,
  honeycrisp, jonagold, or braeburn)
Syrup:
2 cups (475 milliliters) water
3 ½ cups (700 grams) sugar
juice of ½ lemon
½ teaspoon vanilla extract
Filling:
3.5 ounces (103.5 ml) hot milk
1 cup (120 g) ground walnuts
3 tablespoons butter, melted
2 tablespoons sugar
whipped cream

Peel the apples, leaving them whole. Reserve the peels of 2 apples. Discard the rest. Using an apple-corer or a peeler, core the apple about three-quarters of the way down, being sure to remove all seeds. Leave some flesh at the bottom to form a small cup for the filling.

In a pot, combine the water, sugar, vanilla extract, lemon juice, and apple peels. Bring to a boil over high heat, stirring often. Lower the heat to medium, and gently add the apples. Boil the apples for 5 to 7 minutes, turning to make sure both sides get cooked. Cooking time will vary depending on the type and size of the apples. Poke gently with a sharp knife tip or skewer to determine when they are done. They should be soft but not falling apart. Turn off heat. Remove apples from the syrup with a slotted spoon and transfer to a tray to cool down for 30 minutes. Reserve the syrup.

Meanwhile, prepare the filling. In a bowl, cover the ground walnuts with hot milk, and put them aside for 15 minutes. Then add the melted butter and sugar; stir well.

Place apples in serving dishes, cut side up. Fill each apple with 2 to 3 teaspoons of the filling. Pour some syrup over them, and refrigerate until ready to serve. Top with whipped cream.

Adriatic Sea,
  A3—A5, B4—B5,
  C5, D5

Banja Luka, B2
Bihac, A2
Bosna River, C3
Brcko, D2
Busko Jezero, B3

Croatia, A1—A4, B1,
  B3—B5, C1,
  C4—C5, D1—D2

Dalmatian Coast,
  B4
Dinaric Alps, C4, D4
Drina River, D3—D4

Federation of Bosnia
  and Herzegovina,
  A1—A3, B2—B4,
  C2—C5, D2—D4

Kakanj, C3

Lelija (mountain),
  C4

Medjugorje, B4
Montenegro,
  C4—C5, D4—D5
Mostar, C4
Mt. Maglic, C4, D4
Mt. Trebevic, C3

Neretva River, C4

Republika Srpska,
  A1—A2, B1—B3,
  C1—C5, D2—D4

Sarajevo, C3
Sava River, B1
Serbia, D1—D4

Travnik, B3
Tuzla, C2

Vrbas River, B2

Zelengora
  (mountain), C4
Zvornik, D3

ECONOMIC BOSNIA AND HERZEGOVINA

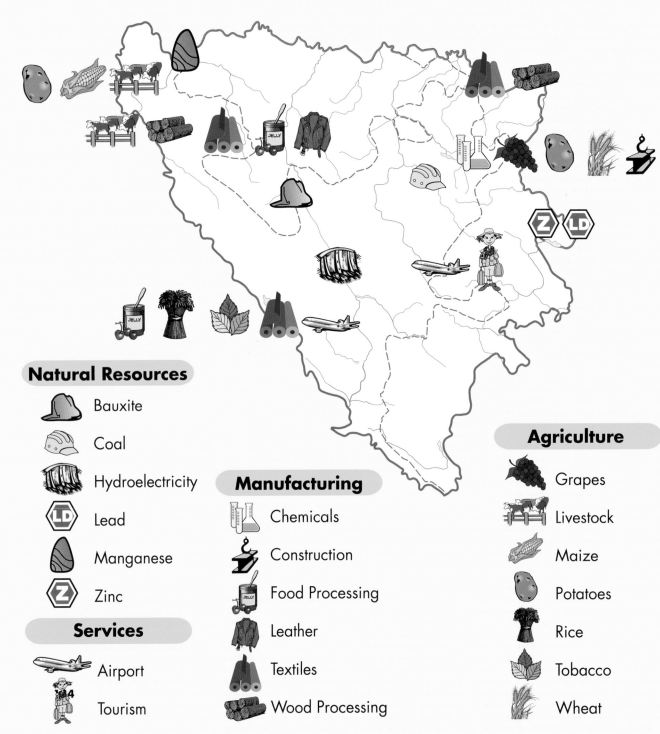

Natural Resources
- Bauxite
- Coal
- Hydroelectricity
- Lead
- Manganese
- Zinc

Services
- Airport
- Tourism

Manufacturing
- Chemicals
- Construction
- Food Processing
- Leather
- Textiles
- Wood Processing

Agriculture
- Grapes
- Livestock
- Maize
- Potatoes
- Rice
- Tobacco
- Wheat

ABOUT THE ECONOMY

All figures are 2017 estimates unless otherwise noted.

GDP (OFFICIAL EXCHANGE RATE)
$18.17 billion

GDP PER CAPITA
$12,800

GDP SECTORS
agriculture: 6.8 percent
industry: 28.9 percent
services: 64.3 percent

CURRENCY
convertible mark, or marka, (BAM)
$1 = 1.76 marks (January 2020)

LABOR FORCE
1.38 million

LABOR FORCE BY OCCUPATION
agriculture: 18 percent
industry: 30.4 percent
services: 51.7 percent

UNEMPLOYMENT RATE
20.5 percent

INFLATION RATE
1.2 percent

AGRICULTURAL PRODUCTS
wheat, corn, fruits, vegetables, livestock

INDUSTRIES
steel, coal, iron ore, lead, zinc, manganese, bauxite, aluminum, motor vehicle assembly, textiles, tobacco products, wooden furniture, ammunition, domestic appliances, oil refining

MAJOR EXPORTS
metals, clothing, wood products

MAJOR IMPORTS
machinery and equipment, chemicals, fuels, foodstuffs

MAIN TRADING PARTNERS
Germany, Croatia, Italy, Serbia, Slovenia, Austria, China, Russia, Turkey

POPULATION BELOW POVERTY LINE
16.9 percent (2015)

CULTURAL BOSNIA AND HERZEGOVINA

Fethija Mosque
The Fethija Mosque in Bihac is an interesting combination of architectural styles in a mosque that was built out of an old Gothic church and retained the tall stained-glass windows.

World War II Memorial
The huge white stones of this memorial in Banja Luka have a solemn dignity. The hill also offers a grand view of the city.

Kastel Fortress
This 16th-century castle on the banks of Vrbas River in Banja Luka hosts a music and drama festival every July.

Dobrinja
This modern suburb was built as the Athletes' Village for the 1984 Winter Olympics.

Gazi Husrev-Beg Mosque
This classic, domed mosque in Sarajevo was built in 1531. The tall minaret was rebuilt due to war damage.

Mount Bjelasnica
This mountain overlooking Sarajevo still has the ski slopes designed for the 1984 Winter Olympics.

Turkish Quarter
The Bascarsija, or Old Turkish Quarter, in Sarajevo has narrow cobblestone streets and is famous for the shops of metalworkers.

Jajce
A medieval fortress looms over the fertile Vrbas River valley. During World War II, this was the headquarters for Tito's Partisan fighters battling the Germans.

Travnik
A medieval fort is the outstanding feature of this small city that was a headquarters for Turkish governors for more than 400 years. This was also the birthplace of Ivo Andric, the great Bosnian novelist.

Apparition Hill
Southwest of Medjugorje, near Podbrdo village, a blue cross marks the spot where six children say they first saw the Virgin Mary.

Karst terrain
In the southern and southwestern parts of BiH, there are deep limestone depressions and caves first described as a karst landscape. The name has since been applied to similar landscapes in other parts of the world.

Stari Most
This bridge in Mostar was built by the Ottoman Turks in 1566, destroyed by Croat artillery in 1993, and rebuilt with international help in 2003.

Turkish House
Still standing after earthquakes and war, this house in Mostar is now nearly 400 years old. It contains Turkish-style rugs and finely carved wooden furnishings.

All figures are 2020 estimates unless otherwise noted.

OFFICIAL NAME
Bosnia and Herzegovina

CAPITAL
Sarajevo

OTHER MAJOR CITIES
Mostar, Banja Luka, Bihac, Gacko, Medjugorge, Travnik

FLAG
Adopted in 1998, the flag shows a yellow triangle on a blue field. The three sides (or points) of the triangle represent the three main ethnic groups—Bosnian Muslims (Bosniaks), Serbs, and Croats. The blue background represents Europe, and the stars stand for the Council of Europe. The two half-stars represent the division of the country into the Federation of Bosnia and Herzegovina and the Serb Republic; these half-stars also represent the hope that the two entities can be united.

POPULATION
3,835,600

POPULATION GROWTH RATE
-0.19 percent

ETHNIC GROUPS
Bosniak 50.1 percent, Serb 30.8 percent, Croat 15.4 percent, other 2.7 percent, not declared/no answer 1 percent (from 2013 census, most recent available)

OFFICIAL LANGUAGES
Bosnian, Serbian, and Croatian

RELIGIONS
Muslim 50.7 percent, Orthodox 30.7 percent, Roman Catholic 15.2 percent, atheist 0.8 percent, agnostic 0.3 percent, other 1.2 percent, undeclared/no answer 1.1 percent (2013)

LIFE EXPECTANCY AT BIRTH
total population: 77.5 years
male: 74.5 years
female: 80.7 years

LITERACY RATE
98.5 percent (2015)

TIMELINE

IN BOSNIA AND HERZEGOVINA	IN THE WORLD
900 The Kingdom of Bosnia is formed.	
1100–1463 Hungarian bans (viceroys) govern Bosnia.	**1054** The Great Schism breaks Christianity into the Roman Catholic and Eastern Orthodox Churches.
1350 The Kingdom of Herzegovina is added to Bosnia; the two are never again separate states.	
1463 Ottoman Turks take control of the region; many South Slavs are converted to Islam.	**1530** The transatlantic slave trade begins, organized by the Portuguese in Africa.
	1776 The US Declaration of Independence is signed.
1875 Bosnia and Herzegovina breaks away from the Ottoman Empire.	**1789–1799** The French Revolution takes place.
1908 Bosnia is annexed to Austria-Hungary.	
1912–1913 Balkan countries fight for their independence.	
1914 Bosnian Serb Gavrilo Princip assassinates Austrian archduke Franz Ferdinand in Sarajevo.	**1914** World War I begins.
1918 Austria-Hungary collapses. Bosnia becomes part of the Kingdom of Serbs, Croats, and Slovenes.	**1917** The Russian Revolution ends the monarchy in Russia.
1941 German troops invade Yugoslavia. The Croatian Ustasa kills Jews and Serbs en masse.	**1939** World War II begins.
1945 Bosnia and Herzegovina becomes a republic within communist Yugoslavia; Tito is in control for 45 years.	**1945** The United States drops atomic bombs on Japan. World War II ends.
1984 The Winter Olympic Games are held in Sarajevo.	**1969** US astronaut Neil Armstrong becomes the first human on the moon.
1991 Croatia, Slovenia, and Macedonia declare their independence from Yugoslavia.	**1991** The Soviet Union breaks up.

IN BOSNIA AND HERZEGOVINA	IN THE WORLD

1992
Bosnia and Herzegovina declares
independence; civil war erupts.

1994
Nelson Mandela becomes president of South Africa.
Genocide and civil war ravage Rwanda.
The Channel Tunnel opens,
connecting Britain and France.

1995
The Srebrenica Massacre kills 8,000 Bosniaks.
NATO begins air strikes against
Bosnian Serb troops.
Leaders of Bosnia, Serbia, and Croatia
sign the Dayton Peace Accords.

1996
The International Criminal Tribunal for the Former
Yugoslavia (ICTY) begins work in The Hague.

1997
Britain returns Hong Kong to China.

2001
The ICTY finds Bosnian Serb general Radislav
Krstic guilty of genocide in the Srebrenica Massacre.

2001
Al-Qaeda terrorists stage 9/11
attacks in the United States.

2006
Former Yugoslav president Slobodan
Milosev dies in The Hague.
Milorad Dodik is elected prime minister
of the Republika Srpska. He remains in
power in different roles indefinitely.

2006
Iraq dictator Saddam Hussein is found guilty of
crimes against humanity in an Iraqi court and
is executed.
Astronomers reclassify Pluto as a dwarf planet.

2008
Former Bosnian Serb leader Radovan
Karadzic is arrested on war crimes charges
after nearly 13 years on the run.

2008
The United States elects its first African
American president, Barack Obama.

2009
An outbreak of H1N1 flu spreads around the world.

2011
Serbian authorities arrest former Bosnian
Serb military chief Ratko Mladic.

2015–2016
ISIS launches terror attacks in Belgium and France.

2016
Bosnia formally applies for EU membership.
The ICTY finds Karadzic guilty of genocide.

2017
The ICTY finds Mladic guilty of genocide.

2017
Hurricanes devastate Houston, Texas;
Caribbean islands; and Puerto Rico.

2018
Dodik wins the Serbian seat on the
three-member federal presidency of BiH.

2019
Notre Dame Cathedral in Paris is damaged by fire.

2020
US president Donald Trump is impeached.

2023
The next BiH census is scheduled to take place.

GLOSSARY

bans (BAHNS)
Viceroys, or governors, sent to rule in the name of the Kingdom of Hungary, but who exercised a good deal of independent control.

bezistan (BEZZ-ih-stahn)
A domed building in Turkish bazaars that housed the shops of craftspeople.

bora
Fierce winds from the north that bring bitterly cold winters to Bosnia.

Bosniaks
Bosnian Muslims.

Brcko (BRITCH-ko) District
A small ethnically mixed municipal region that is an independent entity in BiH.

cevapcici (chay-VAHP-chee-chee)
Sausages stuffed with ground meat and spices, often served with pita bread.

Cyrillic alphabet
An alphabet created in the 800s CE by two brothers, Cyril and Methodius, to help introduce the Bible to South Slavs. It is used by Bosnian Serbs.

dorucak (DOE-ru-chak)
The Bosnian word for "breakfast."

ethnic cleansing
A process in which one ethnic group expels, imprisons, or kills civilians of another ethnic group, usually a minority.

genocide
A deliberate campaign of mass murder for the total destruction of an ethnic, racial, or religious group.

karst region
Areas of limestone outcroppings characterized by jagged depressions, caves, and sinkholes.

Partisans
Yugoslav resistance fighters, including Bosnians, who fought under Marshal Tito to drive out the Germans in World War II.

proteus
Also called an olm, a cave-dwelling salamander-like creature; through centuries of living in complete darkness, it is nearly colorless and has no eyes.

South Slavs
Tribes that settled in the Balkans, including Croatians and Serbs.

Ustasa
The Croatian fascist organization established during World War II; it was responsible for the mass murder of many Serbs, Jews, and Roma.

FOR FURTHER INFORMATION

BOOKS

Filipovic, Zlata. *Zlata's Diary: A Child's Life in Wartime Sarajevo*. New York, NY: Penguin Books, 2006.

Kaplan, Robert D. *Balkan Ghosts: A Journey Through History*. New York, NY: Picador, 2005.

Lippman, Peter. *Surviving the Peace: The Struggle for Postwar Recovery in Bosnia-Herzegovina*. Nashville, TN: Vanderbuilt University Press, 2019.

Reid, Atka, and Hana Schofield. *Goodbye Sarajevo: A True Story of Courage, Love and Survival*. London, UK: Bloomsbury, 2011.

ONLINE

Balkan Insight. https://balkaninsight.com/bosnia-and-herzegovina-home.

BBC News. "Bosnia-Herzegovina Country Profile." https://www.bbc.com/news/world-europe-17211415.

CIA. *The World Factbook*. "Bosnia and Herzegovina." https://www.cia.gov/library/publications/the-world-factbook/geos/bk.html.

Culture Trip. "Bosnia and Herzegovina." https://theculturetrip.com/europe/bosnia-herzegovina.

Lonely Planet. "Bosnia and Hercegovina [sic]." https://www.lonelyplanet.com/bosnia-and-hercegovina.

Sarajevo Times. https://www.sarajevotimes.com.

Srpska Times. http://thesrpskatimes.com.

FILMS

Finding Family. Journeyman Pictures, 2014.

Forgotten Voices, Women in Bosnia. Squeaky Tula Productions, 2008.

Frontline: The Trial of Ratko Mladic. PBS, 2019.

Sarajevo Roses. Igniter Loop, 2017.

Srebrenica: Autoposy of a Massacre. Journeyman Pictures, 2008.

Uspomene 677. Journeyman Pictures, 2012.

MUSIC

Dino Merlin. *Greatest Hits*. Croatia Records/Magaza, 2016.

Dino Merlin. *Hotel Nacional*. Croatia Records/Magaza, 2014.

Divanhana. *Divanhana: Live in Mostar*. Arc Music, 2017.

Various artists. *Bosnia: Echoes From an Endangered World*. Smithsonian Folkways, 1993.

BIBLIOGRAPHY

Balkan Insight. Balkan Transitional Justice section. https://balkaninsight.com/balkan-transitional-justice-home.

BBC News. "Bosnia-Herzegovina Country Profile." https://www.bbc.com/news/world-europe-17211415.

Borger, Julian, et al. "Radovan Karadžić War Crimes Sentence Increased to Life in Prison." *Guardian,* March 20, 2019. https://www.theguardian.com/law/2019/mar/20/radovan-karadzic-faces-final-verdict-in-bosnia-war-crimes-case.

Brezar, Aleksandar. "Bosnia Is Close to the Edge. We Need Europe's Help." *Guardian*, May 29, 2019. https://www.theguardian.com/commentisfree/2019/may/29/bosnia-europe-econmy-ethnic-nationalist.

CIA. *The World Factbook*. "Bosnia and Herzegovina." https://www.cia.gov/library/publications/the-world-factbook/geos/bk.html.

Edwards, Maxim. "The President Who Wants to Break Up His Own Country." *Atlantic*, January 2, 2019. https://www.theatlantic.com/international/archive/2019/01/serb-president-dodik-bosnia/579199.

Freedom House. "Freedom in the World 2019: Bosnia and Herzegovina." https://freedomhouse.org/report/freedom-world/2019/bosnia-and-herzegovina.

Global Security. "Bosnia and Herzegovina (BiH) Introduction." https://www.globalsecurity.org/military/world/europe/ba-intro.htm.

"Is Serbo-Croatian a Language?" *Economist*, April 10, 2017. https://www.economist.com/the-economist-explains/2017/04/10/is-serbo-croatian-a-language.

Khan, Sarah A. "A Journey to Bosnia and Herzegovina, Where Sleeping Beauty Awakens." *New York Times*, May 20, 2019. https://www.nytimes.com/2019/05/20/travel/sarajevo-mostar-muslim-culture.html.

Surk, Barbara. "In a Divided Bosnia, Segregated Schools Persist." *New York Times*, December 1, 2018. https://www.nytimes.com/2018/12/01/world/europe/bosnia-schools-segregated-ethnic.html.

Susnica, Srdan. "Banja Luka: The City of Oblivion and Disdain." *Balkanist*, July 24, 2015. https://balkanist.net/banja-luka-amnesia.

Turp, Craig. "It's Better Than Another War: A Beginner's Guide to Bosnian Politics." *Emerging Europe*, March 8, 2019. https://emerging-europe.com/intelligence/its-better-than-another-war-a-beginners-guide-to-bosnian-politics.

UNESCO Intangible Cultural Heritage. "Bosnia and Herzegovina." https://ich.unesco.org/en/state/bosnia-and-herzegovina-BA.

UNICEF. "Air Quality in Bosnia and Herzegovina." December 12, 2017. https://www.unicef.org/bih/en/clean-air.

INDEX

INDEX